VGM Careers for You Series

CAREERS
FOR
ENVIRONMENTAL
TYPES
& Others Who
Respect the Earth

Mike Fasulo
Jane Kinney

Second Edition

VGM Career Books

Chicago   New York   San Francisco   Lisbon   London   Madrid   Mexico City
Milan   New Delhi   San Juan   Seoul   Singapore   Sydney   Toronto

Library of Congress Cataloging-in-Publication Data

Fasulo, Michael.
    Careers for environmental types & others who respect the Earth / Michael
Fasulo, Jane Kinney.-- 2nd ed.
        p.   cm.   (VGM careers for you series)
        ISBN 0-658-01648-2 (hardcover) -- ISBN 0-658-01649-0 (paperback)
        1. Environmental sciences—Vocational guidance--United States.
I. Title: Careers for environmental types and others who respect the Earth.
II. Kinney, Jane. Careers for environmental types and others who respect the
Earth.   III. Title.   IV. Series.

GE60 .F365   2001
363.7'0023—dc21   2001026433

For my mom, Mary Fasulo,
and sister, Jean Reagan.
In memory of my brother,
Robert Fasulo.

VGM Career Books

A Division of The McGraw·Hill Companies

1 2 3 4 5 6 7 8 9 0   LBM/LBM   0 9 8 7 6 5 4 3 2 1

ISBN 0-658-01648-2 (hardcover)
        0-658-01649-0 (paperback)

This book was set in Goudy Old Style by ImPrint Services.
Printed and bound by Lake Book Manufacturing

McGraw-Hill books are available at special quantity discounts to use as premiums and
sales promotions, or for use in corporate training programs. For more information,
please write to the Director of Special Sales, Professional Publishing, McGraw-Hill, Two
Penn Plaza, New York, NY 10121-2298. Or contact your local bookstore.

This book is printed on acid-free paper.

Contents

Foreword

I grew up on the most polluted lake in the country. At that time—more than thirty years ago—the words *environment* and *environmentalist* had not yet entered our vocabulary in any significant way. I had no idea how the lake got that way, what it meant, or who could help solve the problem. All I knew was that I couldn't swim in the lake, and that seemed very wrong.

Now, of course, an environmental ideology permeates our society. Tens of thousands of community groups address local pollution problems, and many other national and international groups advocate environmental policy. Even some corporations, long seen as the perpetrators of much of the damage, are positioning themselves as caretakers of the environment. Yes, the term *environmentalist* is a vague one, subject to much interpretation and different levels of sincerity. Fundamentally, however, all of us want to do what we can to ensure a healthy environment for all life on the planet.

In my fourteen years as an environmental activist, the same questions came forth: What can I do? Where can I find work in environmental protection? Or in community organizing? Or in governmental environmental policy, corporate acountability, or the environmental sciences? For too long, my answers were neither extensive nor systematic. So, it is a welcome sign that there are now guides to environmental careers, resources that enable people to connect their idealism with employment opportunities.

Today, as our society comes under increasing environmental pressures and risks, all of us, but especially young people, should have the opportunity for jobs whose essence includes the right, if not the duty, to take our conscience to work every day. As you use this resource, keep in mind that what you will bring to these jobs will in no small part help create the future. Be careful in ensuring that the values of the places you may work are compatible with your own values and that you will be allowed to use not only your mind but also your heart.

Peter Bahouth
Greenpeace

CHAPTER ONE

Career Opportunities Today

A s we begin the new millennium, environmental career opportunities are at an all-time high. In no other field today are the opportunities so great and the work so satisfying. Perhaps you are one of the many people who want to do something positive for the Earth and are thinking about making a career of your environmental interests or beliefs. Throughout this book, a rich and rewarding variety of environmental careers will be discussed in detail. This book provides you with a broad overview of the job options existing today in private business, government, the media, and nonprofit organizations, as well as the possibilities for those entrepreneuring types.

The broad cross section of career fields presented, the jobs associated with these fields, and the educational requirements will provide you with a clear and accurate picture of the environmental career landscape. In most instances, you'll find in-depth descriptions of job opportunities and numerous references to other, more detailed information sources. The scope of careers discussed will be helpful to both college students and those who are already in the workforce and are considering a career change. No matter if you are a high school or college student, administrative assistant, customer service representative, lawyer, accountant, or sales agent, there are environmental career paths discussed in this book that may be right for you.

Most environmental career guides written in the last few years talk almost exclusively of scientific and technical environmental jobs. While this job pool is indeed important and discussed throughout this book, the shortfall of these other guides is the scant attention they pay to nonscientific environmental careers. In this book, you'll find career information for science-based environmental careers as well as environmental careers requiring business and liberal arts backgrounds.

While no one book can describe every environmentally focused career or all the components for a successful job search, a well-written and useful career guide will give any reader a better sense of direction and a greater degree of certainty in considering career options. This book will do just that for you!

Environmental Career Types at a Glance

The job opportunities in the environmental field have evolved from their beginnings in the 1960s, when career paths centered exclusively on the conservation sciences, such as natural resource and wildlife management. Today, there is a much greater need for environmental professionals in all sorts of capacities: there are environmental professionals working as engineers, scientists, technicians, educators, entrepreneurs, and marketers, just to name a few. Many environmental professionals have scientific and technical backgrounds, while an increasing number have been trained in business, the humanities, and liberal arts.

Businesslike Types

For those whose interests lie in business, the environmental career opportunities landscape is indeed vast. There are, for example, small companies marketing environmentally friendly products such as clothing and food; medium-size companies manufacturing energy-saving devices and other green technology; and large companies whose business interests span the entire environmental spectrum. In addition, nonprofit organizations are always in need of savvy marketers, and government, at all levels, is in need of business managers.

Scientific Types

For those with an interest in the sciences, the three Rs—remediation (the cleaning up of toxic pollution), recycling (developing collection systems and product machinery), and restoration (managing areas that are recovering from ecological damage)—will provide thousands of new jobs annually. There is a great need for professionals trained in forestry, agriculture, biology, engineering, and botany. Technicians, who outnumber professionals by three to one in most science-oriented fields, are in the highest demand. Technicians are an integral part of any environmental project because they do a majority of the hands-on work.

Liberal Arts Types

Those interested in the social sciences, humanities, or liberal arts are also well represented in the environmental career landscape. There is always a great need for individuals who possess effective communication and organizational skills and who can respond to diverse situations and personalities. Policy analysts, communication specialists, program managers, freelance writers, educators, fund-raisers, copywriters, and lawyers are just a few of the types of environmental professionals in demand.

The Environmental Job Landscape at a Glance

While a major portion of environmental jobs are in the private sector, there are many opportunities in the public and nonprofit sectors as well. The salaries and growth opportunities are as diverse as the types of ecological jobs. Depending on the size and health of the company and economy, the private sector has traditionally been the place with the greatest earning and growth potential. Conversely, the advantage of a public sector career is job security and job-related benefits. Also, both state and federal agencies create and enforce environmental regulations, which along with being a rewarding experience in itself, can also lead to later job opportunities in the private sector. Nonprofit organizations have traditionally lagged in both job security and salaries, but that gap is closing. During the last ten years, the nonprofit sector has enjoyed tremendous growth. There are now thousands of environmental organizations nationwide offering competitive salaries to many new employees each year. Working for nonprofit organizations is very dynamic and exciting, as this is where all the grassroots organizing and community action occurs. As you are beginning to witness, there is truly a place for everyone who is interested in an environmental career.

A Short History of Environmentalism

In the last thirty years, great strides have been made to restore and preserve our environment. In the early 1970s, soon after the activities of the first Earth Day, the American public began to show a great interest in the preservation of our natural world. People finally began to realize that for all the accomplishments that humankind could claim, we have also done great and potentially irreversible damage to the Earth. It suddenly became apparent that our air, water, and soil were quickly becoming poisoned and that we were just beginning to feel the devastating effects. The battle cry was sounded, and the public responded with great resolve. Since the eve of the environmental movement, public concern for the environment has continued to soar.

As a direct result of this intense public concern and pressure, the president and Congress formed the United States Environmental Protection Agency in the early 1970s and since that time, virtually every act of pro-environmental legislation has been enacted. These facts show that the concerns and actions of ordinary individuals can and will make a difference. The people who began the fight for the environment are still going strong, and many more individuals have joined in. As a result of these activities, the number and types of environmental jobs have also grown tremendously.

Environmentalists at Work

We all probably have a common conception of the people we would identify as typical working environmentalists. These individuals tend to be young, carefree, and willing to work hard in low-profile jobs in order to make ends meet. Imagine an environmental activist, with clipboard in hand, going door-to-door soliciting donations. While this type of work offers the ecologically minded canvasser valuable grassroots experience, it is but the tip of the iceberg in terms of the potential pool of environmental careers.

Our stereotypical environmentalist is only one of the many players in the environmental field. In the past thirty years, there has been an explosion of new occupations concerned with the environment. In response to growing public concern about the environment, a whole host of jobs in both the private and public sector have been created or expanded. In this job field there is room for everyone: from those who seek a "conventional job" and wish to climb the career ladder to occupational prestige and job security, to those who prefer jeans and sneakers and the autonomy of being able to work independently. A number of these jobs take place in the structured office environment, while many other are conducted in the outdoors, the courtroom, the office, or a lecture hall.

The career world is full of exciting and rewarding jobs for the ecologically minded. Further, the rewards for choosing an environmental career are quite appealing. Not only will you be doing something personally satisfying, but the contribution that you make will be of net benefit to the Earth. It is only through the work of concerned people like you that we will ensure the continued health of our planet and, just as importantly, a bright and healthy future for our children and future generations.

Types of Environmental Opportunities

Environmental Education

Any discussion of career opportunities must first begin with an emphasis on education. The career paths that we choose or that seem to choose us are largely shaped by our educational experiences. That is why the right education and the ways in which you can match your personal interests with your academic pursuits are extremely important. No matter if you choose a two-year college program, a bachelor's, master's, or even a doctoral degree, there will be a wide variety of environmental careers options available to you.

In response to the increased demand for environmental professionals, many colleges and universities across the nation are designing curricula and degree programs with an environmental focus. In this chapter, traditional majors like forestry and wildlife management will be discussed as well as newer, environmentally focused majors like environmental engineering, public policy, environmental health, environmental law, and interdisciplinary studies. There are outstanding environmental programs at small schools like College of the Atlantic, a nontraditional liberal arts college in Bar Harbor, Maine, and larger universities like the University of California at Santa Barbara, as well as many technical environmental programs at community colleges. In this book, these schools and many others featured will give you a sampling of the many different types of educational experiences. In addition, you will learn strategies for choosing a college, alternative study programs, and the various financial resources available to the college-bound or returning student.

Careers in the Private Sector

Although many environmentalists feel at odds with corporate America, we have made the decision to place the chapter on the private sector near the beginning of this book for two reasons. First, the corporate sector has a unique opportunity because it possesses the greatest human and financial resources to impact positive environmental change. Since private companies are often the culprits in environmental disasters, the placement of well-educated environmentalists at the root of the problem and, thus, the building of a unified front in the war against destructive human practices gives society the greatest weapon in the fight against environmental degradation. Second, this is the job sector in which the greatest number of environmental jobs exists. Given the strong public sentiment about the environment, the corporate sector is under intense pressure to expand the number and profile of environmentally oriented jobs.

Environmental professionals work at the corporate level in a range of areas, including policy making, public relations, overseeing of production and manufacturing, and the overall management of environmental programs. Very often these people are responsible for research into areas of environmental concern, such as implementing and managing work teams, disseminating information to the public, and proposing and fighting for policy changes. Environmental communications specialists and environmental managers are just two types of careers examined indepth later in this book.

Careers in Government

Chapter 4 examines environmental jobs at all levels of government and will focus on some of the major federal environmental branches, such as the Environmental Protection Agency, the National Park Service, and the Forest Service. An environmental career in the government requires a combination of skills and experiences, not the least of which are good communication, flexible thinking, and patience.

Numerous environmental careers exist at the federal level, in dozens of departments, agencies, commissions, and bureaus. The federal government, in response to public environmental concern, is actively deploying teams that are responsible for developing broad regulatory guidelines, overseeing research, providing technical assistance to state and local governments, and supervising the enforcement of environmental regulations.

Federal environmental regulations are passed on to state governments that are responsible for their implementation and enforcement. State governments typically go beyond federal regulations and take initiatives in matters not covered in federal statutes, such as land use, growth planning, and groundwater protection. Numerous state offices and research laboratories carry out specific programs, distribute funds to municipalities, and conduct statewide planning projects.

Because of the increased concern about the state of our environment, the initiative to deal with environmental issues is also increasing at the local level. There are a vast number of jobs at the county and municipal levels. Environmentalists working at the community level usually have hands-on jobs such as inspecting wastewater treatment systems, developing recycling programs, maintaining public land and water-use areas, and mediating between developers and residents. Because of the high turnover rate and hands-on emphasis, this is an excellent place for aspiring environmental professionals to start a career. Entry-level professionals are quickly given substantial responsibility and learn the building-block environmental skills that are useful throughout their careers.

Careers for Eco-Entrepreneurs

The individual with an entrepreneurial spirit has an opportunity to produce, package, or sell items and products that are good for the environment. The eco-entrepreneur, from the environmental artist who creates art from secondhand objects to the environmental vendor who packages or sells goods that are completely recycled or environmentally safe, has a unique opportunity because the public is increasingly concerned with using products that are considered environmentally friendly. In addition, there are an infinite number of possibilities in areas such as recycling, inventing, and providing people with alternatives to chemically laden or wasteful products. There are some wonderful success stories, such as the Body Shop, Tom's of Maine, Ben & Jerry's, and Aveda, that serve as good role models for aspiring eco-entrepreneurs.

Some of these promising career avenues are profiled later in the book along with information and tips on ways to become a successful businessperson. Some resources that may be indispensable to the eco-entrepreneur will also be presented.

Careers in Nonprofit Organizations

One of the best ways to decide whether an environmental career is right for you is to volunteer or intern at an environmental organization. Since there are relatively few staff positions as compared to volunteer positions at environmental organizations, it is prudent for the interested environmentalist to spend some time volunteering or interning with one of these groups. This experience will give you the opportunity to get a feel for the working conditions and atmosphere at nonprofit organizations, and the environmental field in general.

In Chapter 6, some of the larger national environmental organizations will be listed, as will important information on how to get involved with state and local environmental issues and how to pursue volunteering and staff opportunities.

The work done by nonprofit environmental organizations is exciting, and the atmosphere is dynamic. While this is the smallest job sector discussed, in the past ten years, nonprofit environmental organizations and the number of internships, volunteer opportunities, and staff positions has steadily grown.

Careers in Media

The interpretation and dissemination of information has always been a crucial aspect of the democracy in which we live. When important issues are being discussed and decisions are made in the corporate boardroom or at an international environmental conference or on Capitol Hill, it is imperative that citizens have access to information that may have a direct impact on their lives. Choosing a career in the media requires that the individual have a strong ethical perspective and the ability to responsibly investigate and present factual, unbiased information to the general public.

More and more, we are seeing environmental reporters featured on news shows, in newspapers and magazines, and on the Internet. Further, in the last few years, environmental news and information segments have appeared on many local television news programs and on such news and entertainment stations as

MTV, CNN, and A&E. Numerous new books, magazines, and websites focus exclusively on the environment. All types of personnel are needed—including newscasters, writers, editors, camera people, and supporting research staff.

These professions are fast paced, exciting, and personally rewarding, with new opportunities arising daily. Whether you are the environmental reporter for the *New York Times* or for the local television station, your impact is potentially enormous. There is a large and growing audience that wants to be educated on environmental issues. In addition, beyond the confines of your desk, the opportunity for freelancing your writing skills is also growing. With initiative and resourcefulness, a media environmentalist can earn a handsome living.

Is an Environmental Career Really for You?

One of the first steps in making a major decision like choosing or changing a career path is to examine your motives and assess your qualifications. Here are some questions you may want to ask yourself:

1. Do I already consider myself to be an environmentalist? Is my lifestyle consistent with my environmental beliefs?

2. What activities have I participated in that are related to the environment?

3. Is the integration of my values and ethics into my career a priority for me?

4. What type of work interests me—lab work, sales, production, education and training, policy making, planning, or something else entirely?

5. What type of work environment do I want to be a part of? Do I want to work primarily in an office or out in the field? Am I more comfortable working as part of a team or as an individual?

6. Do I prefer to work on long-term projects, or do I prefer a more loosely defined job with mainly short-term projects and diverse day-to-day tasks?

7. Do I prefer working in an urban or rural setting?

8. Am I willing to travel?

9. Am I willing to relocate to areas where jobs are available?

10. Can I live on a modest but comfortable income, or do I want to quickly climb the financial ladder?

11. Am I willing to go through years of postsecondary education and/or technical training?

It would be a good idea to write down your answers to these questions to get you thinking about what kind of career and lifestyle you really desire. In order to be truly satisfied with any career, it is essential to first understand yourself and what motivates and excites you. You will be spending a substantial portion of your waking hours at your job; therefore, a good match between your personality characteristics and job requirements will make your career a much more satisfying one.

CHAPTER TWO

Environmental Education

O ne of the most vital components in making your environmental career a successful one is choosing the correct course of study. This applies not only to recent high school graduates who are considering a college education but also to individuals who have turned their professional attention toward an environmental career. In many organizations today, environmental literacy is becoming a managerial requisite.

The good news is that environmental employment opportunities are at an all-time high. During the past twenty years, there has been a sharp increase in the number of companies hiring environmental professionals. According to the Department of Commerce, there are more than seventy thousand environmentally focused companies, organizations, and government agencies. Also, a recent study at the University of California, Los Angeles, found that 83 percent of all college freshmen "want to make a positive contribution to the environment" and 21 percent "want to work on environmental issues." Couple this with the fact that each year thousands of people with solid professional experience are switching to environmentally oriented careers, and the job picture zooms into focus and suggests that anyone interested in pursuing an environmental career should seriously consider the educational requirements in today's workforce. It doesn't matter if your education, interests, or work background are in the humanities or the basic sciences. There are English majors heading hazardous-waste cleanup firms, political scientists setting state and federal recycling policy, engineers developing and marketing high-efficiency industrial equipment, biologists leading international conferences on world resources conservation, business majors forming their own companies or working at non-profit environmental organizations. What made the difference for these people is that they knew how to make the best of their education and skills to find deeply satisfying careers.

Recent Trends in Environmental Education

There are some recent trends in the environmental job sector that deserve particular attention. First, a college degree is becoming a standard prerequisite for employment. This is a solid requirement for young, entry-level applicants and a definite edge for those with established job experience. A four-year bachelor's degree is becoming the norm for most professional job candidates, while a two-year associate's degree or certificate of training from a community college or vocational institute is the prerequisite for most technical positions.

Further, it is also not unusual for employers to hire a large number of candidates with some form of graduate training. Increasingly, private companies and government agencies are requiring, as a condition of employment, that their employees take continuing environmental education courses. These classes are partially or fully paid for by an employer and often lead to a technical certificate or even a graduate degree. The reason for these rigorous educational standards is quite simple: the complexity of environmental problems and the level of technological and organizational sophistication necessary to solve our most pressing environmental problems make those with a postsecondary education and a willingness to keep on learning the most attractive job candidates.

Second, a basic understanding of the physical sciences for all career-minded environmentalists is becoming essential. This may not be a problem for some people but there are others for whom just the utterance of the words *math* and *science* sends a chill straight up their spines. Remember, there is a big difference between an understanding of scientific issues and the pursuit of a degree in the "hard" sciences. By definition, ecology is the study of ecosystems, the relation of living organisms to their environments. An understanding of the principles of this relationship is essential in order to grasp the complexity of environmental problems. There is ample room in this field for both generalists who may be involved in policy decisions, fundraising, or public education and specialists who design specific systems or explore particular scientific ideas, problems, and solutions. Each person should, however, have a solid understanding of environmental issues and be able to verbalize how humans have caused harm to the environment and how we can work to solve these problems.

There is presently a career advantage for those whose education leans toward the physical sciences. At present, a majority of environmental job descriptions stress some type of specific scientific training. This heavily biased emphasis on training in the sciences does, however, appear to be giving way to a more integrated approach, incorporating both the physical and social sciences. A combination of scientific, communication, and business skills is beginning to define the ideal environmental career; those best able to synthesize these skills will be highly sought after. One college brochure describing its environmental science program states this case:

> Society needs specialist biologists, geologists and geographers, and will continue to do so in the foreseeable future. Society also needs generalist environmental scientists who can coordinate and interpret data emanating from widely differing disciplines. This is

vital if [humanity] is to take the necessary steps to halt the cur-
rent over-exploitation of the Earth, and is to attempt to meet the
demands of a human population far in excess of ecological bal-
ance... it is desirable that a higher proportion of our future politi-
cians and administrators should make environmental science,
rather than an arts subject, their basic education.

Finally, increasing attention is being paid to prospective employees with good reasoning and communication skills. These liberal arts tools include analytical thinking, writing, speaking, and cooperative abilities. While these are the strengths of most students interested in the humanities, they have historically been a weakness for those trained in the physical sciences. Increasingly, employers are looking for people who have a substantive understanding of technical issues and who can come up with creative solutions and, most importantly, relate their ideas to others. In the Environmental Career Organization's *Complete Guide to Environmental Careers*, the vice president of a large timber firm pointedly addressed this issue, saying, "What separates the forest managers from the technicians is not their knowledge of forestry but their liberal arts skills: They can work with people, they can communicate and they can see and solve problems."

Sources of Information

Careers in the Environment, 2nd ed. (2000). By Michael Fasulo and Paul Walker and published by VGM Career Books. Contains an excellent discussion of educational requirements including traditional and nontraditional college programs and advanced certificate programs. It also emphasizes extracurricular environmental activities such as summer work programs, volunteer and internship organizations.

Careers for Nature Lovers & Other Outdoor Types, 2nd ed. (2000). By Louise Miller and published by VGM Career

Books. Includes information on careers in the biological sciences, agricultural sciences, land planning, forestry and conservation science, geology, and pollution control and waste management.

The Complete Guide to Environmental Careers in the 21st Century (1999). By the Environmental Careers Organizaton and published by Island Press. An excellent resource for scientific and technical careers that includes a good discussion of both formal and informal educational information.

The Basics: A Good High School Education

You can start to prepare for your environmental career long before choosing a college major or trying to convince an interviewer, while squirming in your chair and picking imaginary lint from your clothing, that you are the perfect job candidate. This doesn't mean that you must know your exact career ambitions by the time you enter or leave high school. It does imply that you should take your high school education seriously and use it to your advantage later in life. Many of the basics taught in junior high and high school will make your college experience easier and more rewarding. Those with the best college experiences, in terms of not only grades but also the development of a healthy self-esteem and intellectual curiosity, will surely stand out among the career-seeking crowd.

First, a solid grasp of math and English are really the golden keys to your educational and career success. Mathematics is the foundation of all the sciences and is an indispensable skill for any career-minded environmentalist. You should take a full four years of high school math with two years of algebra, one year of geometry and trigonometry, and at least one year of calculus. The communication arts—reading, writing, and speech—are equally important. No matter what you later choose as a field of study or occupation, it cannot be overstressed that English skills are an essential part of the formula for professional success. You should take, in addition to the required English classes, litera-ture, composition, and public-speaking courses.

All young, environmentally minded students are advised to take high school courses that offer a wide variety of environ-mental/scientific information. Classes in biology, the earth sci-ences, physics, and chemistry are a good start. Along with helping you understand complex issues such as hazardous waste problems, global warming, and ozone depletion, these courses will prepare you for similar but much more challenging college classes. Finally, talk to your guidance counselor about your inter-ests so he or she can help you design a plan of study.

Choosing the Right College

Unlike other fields of study, such as English, engineering, soci-ology, or education, environmental studies traditionally did not fit neatly or exclusively into one academic department. Only very recently, mainly in reaction to a growing student interest in envi-ronmental studies, have colleges created environmental programs within academic departments or interdisciplinary programs that combine the teachings of different fields.

In the past few years, educators have been seriously interested in creating more of these types of programs. Unfortunately, ongoing budget problems have forced many schools to scale back existing programs and defer or cancel new programs altogether. While there is a need for a greater variety of environmental pro-grams, it appears that the demand will outpace the supply for at least the next few years. Fortunately, there are already a large number of programs throughout the country to choose from.

Some Important Issues

It would be nice if all applicants could find the environmental program and school that fit their needs exactly, but, unfortunately, this is not always the case. Whether you are a first-time or returning student, you will be faced with making important and often life-altering decisions for the sake of your education. The pursuit of a higher education requires you to commit a sizeable amount of time, energy, and money in return for a degree that will open new, exciting career doors. Most of us would love to attend the best school, remain near our friends and family, make outstanding grades, and have ample time to study and socialize. Not very often, though, are all of these wishes realistic or even possible. Before researching and collecting information on schools, it would help to consider these three questions to better understand what you are looking for in a school and environmental program.

1. What type of environmental training do you really want or need? This is probably your most important consideration in choosing the right school and/or educational track. Do you want a full four-year degree at a university where you will be required to take a wide range of courses in the humanities and "hard" sciences and gain a broad understanding of environmental issues, or do you want a more specific technical or scientific education in two years or less?

2. How much do you want to spend on your education? In general, the least expensive schools are community colleges

and technical institutions. Public four-year colleges and universities occupy the middle price range, and private schools tend to be the most costly. Also, it is usually much less expensive to attend a public college or technical school in your own state. Students from other states are typically charged twice the amount or more than state residents.

3. Would you be comfortable at a large university where classes are large and the atmosphere is somewhat impersonal yet exciting, or would you feel better attending a smaller school where classes are small and the atmosphere is more sedate?

Answering these questions will help you choose the kind of learning environment that is right for you and will aid you in choosing the type of school in which you feel the most comfortable.

Two-Year Schools: A Technical Environmental Education

Two-year colleges are a convenient, affordable, and rewarding way to continue your education and are often a direct conduit to an environmental job. The term *two-year school* is an umbrella term for junior and community colleges, private occupational schools, area vocational schools, adult education centers, and correspondence schools. These schools enroll more than six million students per year, or 40 percent of all college students. The reason for this high enrollment rate is quite simple: our technological society demands a large number of highly skilled workers to keep it functioning. For every one professional job in the environmental sciences, for example, there are three technicians employed.

These schools differ from four-year liberal arts colleges primarily in that they are oriented to teach students specific skills that are directly related to employment opportunities. Two-year schools are also a good choice for those who don't feel that the academic program at a four-year college is quite right for them. For example, high school students who are absorbed in one subject like science, mechanics, or the arts, returning students who are seeking further training or a certification for a specific job, or individuals looking to be retrained in order to change careers are all well suited for this type of education.

Tuition at two-year public schools is one-half or less than tuition at public four-year colleges and an eighth of the cost of private colleges. Further, many two-year schools have open-door admission policies that make them accessible to everyone. Also, these colleges are community based, which makes them convenient for students who need to maintain a close link with family or employers.

Unlike four-year colleges, where you may be forced to travel far to find a specific program, two-year schools are much more numerous, and the chances of finding just the right program close to home are quite good. Most community colleges also offer liberal arts transfer curricula that prepare students with the first two years of courses, after which they can transfer to a four-year school and receive a bachelor's degree.

In the environmental field, workers with many forms of technical training are in high demand. In the areas of solid waste management, hazardous waste management, air and water quality, and land and water conservation, just to name a few, there are presently a shortage of qualified technicians. Further, the work generated by the Superfund hazardous and toxic waste cleanup program, military base closures, and local pollution control efforts will ensure the continuing need for qualified workers for many years to come.

Sources of Information

Peterson's Guide to Two-Year Colleges (annual). Published by
Peterson's Guides. Lists more than thirty majors that are
related to the environment and includes a two-page
description of most schools.

Occupational Outlook Handbook (2000–2001). By the U.S.
Department of Labor and published by VGM Career Books.
The definitive source of statistical career information.
Contains references to hundreds of technical careers.

An Insider's Guide to Success in the Two-Year College (1999).
By Gary Sattelmeyer and published by Barron's Educational
Series. Describes strengths and weaknesses specific to two-
year colleges and discusses getting financial aid, planning
and scheduling courses, developing good study habits and
critical thinking skills, getting the most from counselors and
faculty, transferring academic credits, and setting career
goals.

Environmental Learning:
The Traditional College Major

Environmental courses are sewn into a wide range of educational
offerings; many of these programs offer a high quality education
and, above all, the benefit of a college and program that is established, respected, and, thus, marketable. Typically, students
receive either a bachelor of arts or a bachelor of science degree
and choose a major course of study in one academic department.

Peterson's Guide to Four-Year Colleges lists forty different
academic majors with an environmental focus. According to

Barron's *Profiles of American Colleges*, more than 230 four-year schools offer an undergraduate major in environmental studies. The bulk of these programs are in environmental science and are rooted in the basic sciences, but many have an interdisciplinary focus.

In addition, there are more than twenty-five degree programs specifically in environmental engineering. In the social sciences, there are somewhat fewer environmental degree offerings. Fifteen colleges offer a degree program in environmental design, and three confer environmental education degrees. There are, however, many interdisciplinary programs in public policy, geography, sociology, and rural sociology.

Some Popular Environmental Majors

The agricultural sciences focus on the study of plants and animals. Environmentally focused majors include fish and game management, forestry, animal and food science, natural resource management, range management, and soil science.

The biological sciences concentrate on the study of all living organisms—from humans to microbes to their life processes and evolutionary development—and offer environmentally focused programs in biochemistry, microbiology, molecular biology, ecology, zoology, marine biology, and botany.

The earth sciences examine the processes that created, sustain, and change the Earth. Degree offerings include chemistry, geology, geography, physics, meteorology, and oceanography.

In engineering, students learn to apply mechanical principles to practical situations using tools and machines. Environmental engineering is defined by the American Academy of Environmental Engineers as "The management and optimum use of air, water and land resources, and the provision of facilities and the control of conditions for living, working and recreation that will contribute positively to human health, comfort and well-being."

Surveyors, architects, and landscapers work closely with engineers and help design and implement environmental projects.

A host of liberal arts departments have integrated environmental issues into their curricula. In sociology, political science, psychology, human geography, public policy and administration, education, and business, the focus is on the behavioral aspects of human impact on the environment. Individuals with social science backgrounds often manage environmental projects and conduct policy research.

There are also environmentally focused majors in the health sciences, including public health specialists, sanitary engineers, occupational hygienists, emergency/disaster scientists, and toxicologists, to name just a few.

Sources of Information

The following four-year college directories are available at libraries and high schools and in the reference section of many bookstores. You can also search the Internet by typing the keywords *environmental education*.

Peterson's Guide to Four Year Colleges (annual). Published by Peterson's Guides, Princeton NJ.

Profile of American Colleges (annual). Published by Barron's Educational Service, Inc.

Lovejoy's College Guide (annual). Published by Prentice Hall.

Index of Majors (annual). Published by the College Entrance Examination Board, New York.

Interdisciplinary College Majors

There has been a move in many schools to bring together faculty from different departments to form interdisciplinary environmental programs. The purpose of these programs is to integrate the teachings of various disciplines and present the student with a more complete or holistic understanding of environmental issues. Remember, the definition of ecology, with its emphasis on the interrelation of humans to the environment, suggests that the social and physical sciences be pulled together and studied simultaneously. In this vein, for example, it makes little sense to study solutions to air pollution exclusively from an engineering standpoint. To do so would disregard the importance of the economic, social, or political factors, all of which influence the outcome of any program designed to reduce air pollution. It may be technically feasible to place scrubber devices on all smokestacks and drastically curtail the amount of toxins released into the air, but it may be difficult, if not impossible, to get companies to actually install them without government regulations. What appears as a rather simple task from an engineering standpoint is actually a quite challenging objective when considered in the economic and political realm.

The intent of interdisciplinary programs is to overcome the shortfalls of unidimensional classroom learning. A course that considers the subject of air pollution control would have economists, sociologists, and political scientists, as well as engineers, explaining their various approaches to the problem and would give the student a more realistic conception of how environmental problems are approached and solved. This combination of technical, social, political, and economic teachings is at the core of many environmental programs.

Some large universities have developed solid interdisciplinary environmental curricula. Pennsylvania State University, through the cooperation of the departments of meteorology, geology, and geography, operates the Earth Systems Science Center. At the State University of New York at Syracuse, the College of Forestry and Environmental Science has built a strong reputation. The University of North Carolina at Chapel Hill has built its Department of Environmental Science and Engineering into one of the finest programs in the country. Indiana University at Bloomington offers environmental studies in both the College of Liberal Arts and the School of Public and Environmental Affairs. Illinois State University at Normal has an environmental health program that integrates medical and public policy issues. Also, the University of California at Santa Barbara has a fine environmental studies curriculum in its School of Liberal Arts.

Small and Innovative Environmental Schools

A number of schools offer an alternative educational experience where students are encouraged to be independent and creative thinkers and are individually guided to pursue the environmental ideas and issues that interest them most. Many of these environmental colleges were established in the 1960s and 1970s, during the first big wave of social environmentalism, and their continued success exemplifies a deep commitment to environmental values shared by succeeding generations.

Students are motivated by curiosity rather than grades, and a good number of these schools have done away with the rigid grading system altogether, in favor of faculty and peer review of student progress. Learning is demonstrated through small group interactions, individual projects, fieldwork, and internships. The major advantage of these small and focused schools is the deep commitment to teaching rather than a focus on faculty research.

The following is only a sampling of the many educational institutions that have respected programs and motivated and dedicated students and faculty.

Prescott College

Prescott College is nestled in the wooded mountains of central Arizona in a small, close-knit community that provides students with a healthy atmosphere and a strong sense of "commitment to responsible participation in the natural environment and human community," according to the college's general catalog. This is a small school with a little more than five hundred students living on and around the campus. Prescott College offers bachelor of arts degrees in environmental studies, human development and education, outdoor education and leadership, cultural and regional studies, and humanities. During the first month of residency, all new students participate in a three-week wilderness expedition designed to teach environmental ethics and reverence for the planet. There is also an adult degree program through which adult students can earn a bachelor or master of arts degree in liberal arts fields including education, counseling, management, psychology, and human services. Students complete their degrees in their own communities, and the only residency requirement is two weekends at the Prescott campus. For more information about the college, write to:

Prescott College
220 Grove Avenue
Prescott, AZ 86301

College of the Atlantic

College of the Atlantic is a four-year, independent college located on Mount Desert Island in Bar Harbor, Maine. The campus consists of twenty-six shorefront acres adjacent to Acadia National Park and overlooks Frenchman Bay. The school offers both bachelor of arts and master of arts degrees in human ecology. The teaching of the interconnection of humans with their physical surroundings is a central mission of the college. The curriculum is split into three areas of concentration: environmental science, arts and design, and human studies. The college has a strong concentration of classes in marine biology, environmental design, environmental media, and education. Undergraduate requirements include at least two courses in each area of concentration, a human ecology essay, an internship, a senior project, and community service. The master's program is a more intensive extension of the undergraduate program, and many students who enter the program continue with their undergraduate focus.

There is a cooperative agreement between the college and Acadia National Park, through which students conduct much of their fieldwork in the park. The college also maintains the Island Research Center, where "students monitor populations of endangered or threatened bird species, develop censusing techniques for bird populations, and observe the impact of changes in island vegetation on animal species," according to the college bulletin. For more information, write to:

College of the Atlantic
105 Eden Street
Bar Harbor, ME 04609

The Evergreen State College

The Evergreen State College is a four-year public school tucked away in the rolling and forested mountains of Olympia, Washington. This is one of the very few state schools that has both an alternative curriculum and an environmental focus. Evergreen offers both bachelor of arts and bachelor of science degrees, as well as a master's degree in environmental studies. The environmental studies program stresses the interaction of human societies and nature. The goals of this program are:

- To understand the nature, development, and interactions of terrestrial and marine ecosystems and human societies

- To learn the richness and the limits of the environment and social resources available to sustain both human environments and natural systems

- To study the cultural values and philosophies that shape environmental behavior and, through applied work, to develop the skills necessary to handle our resources wisely

The environmental studies program also maintains a close link to the programs in political economy, social change, science, technology, and health. The master's program combines public policy and environmental science so that graduates can use a combination of management and technical skills.

A student's academic pathway is at first structured, with a number of core program requirements, but later becomes more independent and specialized. Instead of grades, faculty members write a narrative evaluation of each student's work, and, in turn, students prepare self-evaluations and also evaluations of the instructors. Thus, Evergreen stresses learning through an open and honest two-way communication system between faculty and students. Further information can be obtained from:

Administrative Office
The Evergreen State College
Olympia, WA 98505

Also of Note

Other notable small, environmentally focused alternative colleges include Hampshire College in Amherst, Massachusetts; Northland College in Ashland, Wisconsin; Colorado Mountain College in Leadville, Colorado; and the Huxley College of Environmental Studies, a unit of Western Washington University in Bellingham, Washington.

Environmental Study Alternatives: Making Your Own Major

While there are indeed many more degree programs in environmental studies today as opposed to ten years ago, finding a school that matches both your interests and needs may still be a big challenge. A student interested in an environmental engineering program may find that there are none in his or her state, or someone interested in both ecology and public policy may have trouble finding a school that has such a joint program. In addition, students are often faced with making difficult lifestyle compromises. Colleges that have an established environmental studies program may be far from home or too expensive and, thus, not a practical choice. When faced with this dilemma, some may decide to compromise and choose a program that isn't quite what they wanted.

A good alternative, which requires a flair for creativity and a little self-motivation, is to design your own special environmental major. In this case, it is up to you to seek out schools in your area that have the relevant environmental courses, to create a class schedule for each term, and to meet all the course requirements of the school. Many schools permit this type of flexible scheduling, especially when the student has specific interests and goals.

There are usually a number of faculty members at any school pursuing environmental issues. It would be wise to find out who these faculty members are and contact them to see if you have similar interests. Also, make sure that they are interested in what you want to do and, most importantly, that they have the time to help you. Contact the dean's office or the office of student affairs to see if this type of arrangement is possible.

Graduate Schools

Graduate training is far and away the most popular trend for workers in the business world today. For example, how many people do you know or have you heard of who have a master of business administration (M.B.A.) degree or are planning on attending graduate school? Just a few years ago, holders of advanced degrees were the exception, while now they are becoming the norm.

The environmental field is ripe for professionals with advanced educational training. This field has experienced tremendous growth in the past ten years and requires individuals with advanced scientific training and modern management skills.

A recent survey of environmental cleanup firms found that an increasing number of their new professional employees have advanced degrees in fields like biology, engineering, chemistry, and business administration. In addition, nonprofit environmental organizations are hiring a large number of both scientists and policy analysts with graduate degrees.

Graduate school can be a wonderful learning experience and very helpful for your career, but you should think long and hard about your motivations for wanting a graduate degree and the type of degree and training you hope to receive. Unlike most undergraduate programs, which have their core subject matter and offer a general learning experience, graduate programs are intensive and specific.

If you have just finished your undergraduate education and are torn between going directly to graduate school or first getting some work experience, consider that most college faculty find that returning students are generally more focused and successful because their studies are tied directly to their careers. This doesn't mean that you should not go directly from undergraduate to graduate school, but today many students enter graduate school as if it were an extension of their undergraduate training, with little if any idea of what they would like to do after completing their degrees.

Far and away, the most complete and detailed information source on graduate programs is *Peterson's Annual Guide to Graduate Study*, which comes in six separate guides and gives a detailed description of schools, programs, departments, faculty, and the present academic focus.

1. *Graduate and Professional Programs, Overview*

2. *Humanities, Arts, and the Social Sciences*

3. *Biological Sciences*

4. *Physical Sciences, Mathematics, Agricultural Sciences, the Environment, and Natural Resources*

5. *Engineering and Applied Sciences*

6. *Business, Education, Health, Information Studies, Law, and Social Work*

You can also find valuable information in the *Guide to Graduate Environmental Programs* (1997), published by the Student Conservation Association.

A Cautionary Note on Graduate Programs

While the need for integrated environmental learning is well recognized outside the world of academia, there is still quite a bit of resistance to forming interdisciplinary programs at our institutes of higher learning, especially in graduate programs. The reason for this is unfortunately quite simple: many professors consider interdisciplinary studies as academically inferior to the work done in their own disciplines. Call it a form of academic xenophobia, but theory has it that incorporating other subjects into a discipline somehow waters it down and makes the work less respectable. This stigma also carries over to students. Their broad academic interests are viewed as academically diluted, and the students themselves are often viewed as being less bright than their more specialized counterparts who study a single subject. This is not the norm in all graduate programs, but it is something to be aware of. When researching graduate programs, make it clear that you seek additional training for professional reasons and that you are not interested in a career in academia, where the stigma is strongest.

Law Schools

In recent years, the battle against environmental degradation has increasingly been taking place in the courts of law. In the 1980s, environmentalists, frustrated with political foot dragging in the enforcement and reauthorization of environmental regulations, looked to the courts for protection. The result of all this activity was a huge increase in litigation and the need for a larger corps of lawyers with environmental training. However, there are still only a handful of law schools that offer training in environmental law.

Northwestern Law School of Lewis & Clark College

Northwestern Law School of Lewis & Clark College is a fully accredited law school located in Portland, Oregon. Northwestern has an environmental and natural resource program in which more than a third of the school's students participate. To earn a certificate and claim a concentration in environmental and natural law, students are required to take, in addition to their required classes, several courses in environmental law and to write two publishable papers. Also, *Environmental Law*, a journal devoted to environmental law issues, is published at the school. Many of Northwestern's graduates go on to work for national environmental groups like the National Resource Defense Council, for governmental agencies, and in socially conscious private law practices. For further information, contact:

Northwestern Law School
Department of Admissions
Lewis & Clark College
10015 Southwest Terwilliger Boulevard
Portland, OR 97219

University of Colorado Law School

The University of Colorado Law School, located at the foot of the Rocky Mountains in Boulder, Colorado, established the Natural Resource Law Center in 1981 because of the steady rise in legislation and regulations regarding natural resources. The center hosts educational programs for scholars, government officials, public interest groups, and members of industry, as well as sponsoring distinguished visitors and supporting research and publications pertaining to natural resources. While the center sponsors no formal educational program in the law school, students gain constant access and have the opportunity to foster professional relationships with practicing lawyers and scholars who deal with natural resource issues. For information, contact:

Natural Resources Law Center
University of Colorado School of Law
Campus Box 401
Boulder, CO 80309

Sources of Information

Barron's Guide to Law Schools (annual). Published by Barron's Educational Service, Inc. Contains information on environmental law programs and the way to prepare for law school as an undergraduate.

Association of American Law Schools, 1201 Connecticut Avenue NW, Washington, DC 20036. Write for a listing of accredited law schools with environmental programs.

Financial Aid

The cost of a college education has more than doubled in the last ten years and is expected to keep rising in the coming decade. It was not long ago that only students interested in private schools or specialized programs like law and medicine had to factor in cost as a deciding factor of college attendance because the vast network of public schools offered a high quality education at an affordable cost. This simply is no longer the case. According to the *Princeton Review*, in 2001, the average cost of a year's tuition, room and board, and fees will be $9,525 at a typical four-year public college and $23,208 at private schools. By 2010, this figure is expected to rise to about $16,000 per year at public schools and $36,000 per year at private colleges.

Student Loans and Grants

Loans and scholarships are the two main sources of financial aid available to all students. Student loans are relatively straightforward and easy to secure. Almost every school has a financial aid office or representative where you can get information on the amount and terms of loans, as well as help with filling out the required forms. The majority of students seeking money for school use these loans as their main sources of financial aid. The largest loan programs in the country are the federal Perkins, Stafford, and PLUS loan programs. Student loan programs once had the reputation of being a source of easy money because many students simply did not repay their loans. The government and banks are now, however, much more strict with their lending policies.

The federal Pell Grant is the largest grant program, with almost four million students receiving a Pell Grant each year. This grant is intended to be the starting point of financial aid assistance for lower-income families.

Scholarships

Scholarships are money given, not lent, to students. Money is granted to those who, on the basis of need or merit, meet the requirements of the granting body. There are literally thousands of organizations with scholarship funds throughout the United States, and every year thousands of individual scholarships, worth millions of dollars, go unused simply because no one bothered to apply for them.

Many students are under the incorrect impression that scholarships are only for the poor and academically or physically gifted. You can receive a scholarship because of particular interests such as writing, reading, or hobbies; the geographic area in which you were raised; special skills; language abilities; mechanical inclinations; and so forth.

For just about any human ability, there is a scholarship out there somewhere just waiting to be awarded. At Juniata College in Pennsylvania, for example, left-handers compete annually for a $20,000 grant left by a southpaw couple. Volunteers for the Student Union Social Committee at the University of Wisconsin who were raised in the New York area are eligible for a $500 scholarship each year. There are perhaps thousands of scholarships created specifically for the study of environmental problems.

There are no universal standards for scholarships; the amount of financial award depends solely upon the granting organization. In general, most scholarships range from $50 to $1,000, while some even pay full tuition costs. There is no one listing of scholarships or their sources, and, consequently, the most difficult part of receiving a scholarship is just finding out about it. You can either do the research on your own or use a scholarship search service. These services typically charge $50 to $100 per search and have the advantage of being able to narrow the scholarship search specifically to awards that highlight your personal strengths and specific sources of environmental funding.

Sources of Information

The Internet can provide a good starting point in your search for scholarship information. Use the keywords *college scholarships* to begin, or you can search the specific websites of the colleges you are interested in attending. More information can be found in the following resource books, often available at school and community library reference desks.

The Scholarship Book (annual). Published by Prentice Hall. A
    complete guide to private-sector scholarships, loans, and
    grants for undergraduates. There is a section on funding for
    environmental studies and lists of scholarship guides.

Peterson's Scholarships, Grants and Prizes (annual). Published by Peterson's Guides. Offers an extensive listing of additional sources of financial aid for students.

For More Information

Educational Resource Information Center (ERIC). Sponsored by the U.S. Department of Education, ERIC is a database that provides computer access to information dealing with education. This system includes more than ten thousand documents dealing with environmental education. Check at local colleges and high schools for access to ERIC.

Conservation Directory (annual). Published by the National Wildlife Federation. Included in this potpourri of environmental information is a chapter on colleges and universities with environmental programs.

World Environmental Directory (annual). Published by Business Publishers, Inc. This large reference manual includes entries on environmental education programs, databases, and funding sources.

CHAPTER THREE

Careers in the Private Sector

A s our concern for the environment continues to grow, many new challenges and opportunities have arisen for individuals and corporations that have not traditionally concerned themselves with the environment. This rising concern about the environment and an increased awareness of the environmental impact of corporate actions by consumers, legislators, and executives, coupled with more and stricter environmental regulations, is forcing companies to rethink their manufacturing, production, and management strategies. The challenges lie in integrating environmental policies without losing jobs and drastically reducing profits, and in reshaping the thinking of corporate and industrial America as it exists today. The opportunities can be found in new emerging markets for environmentally conscious products and increased employment in environmental industry.

The integration of environmental ethics into jobs such as banking, law, and marketing, which have traditionally been disinterested or hostile to environmental interests, has created a host of new opportunities. People can now combine concern for the Earth's natural resources with an interest in business. Across the country, new positions, new divisions, and new industries are emerging. An environmentally literate manager enhances decision making and ultimately designs and implements policies that will provide a new framework for management policies and successful businesses. An environmentally conscious retailer will respond to consumers' requests for "green" products by developing and marketing products that have been produced without harming the Earth.

Environmental awareness is starting to become an integral part of mainstream corporate culture and will continue to do so. The environment must be considered in the daily decisions of employees and managers in a wide variety of areas, from purchasing, packaging, research and development, marketing, sales, and training to public relations. The division that has existed between the "environmentalists" and the "polluters" since the beginning of the industrial revolution has begun to close, and numerous opportunities are available for those who are willing to close the gap even further.

The new corporate employee is a "green-collar" worker, one who can connect personal values about the environment with professional interests. People with expertise in the sciences, finance, management, policy making, and communications are increasingly finding jobs that combine their interests and skills. For the job seeker with the right education, experience, and commitment, the financial rewards can be significant.

Opportunities in Green Corporate America

The following list of opportunities for employment in a greener corporate America is designed to give you a general idea of where new positions are being created in response to the demand for greater control over environmental issues. As you will note, an environmental factor is present in almost every aspect of business, and your knowledge of environmental issues coupled with expertise in any given area will make you an ideal candidate to become part of the greening of our nation's businesses.

Public Sector

This group involves federal, state, and local government officials who have the responsibility of regulating industry, allocating resources for cleanup, defending the environment, solving environmental problems, and a number of other specialty professions.

Private Sector

Private interest groups, labor groups, and other not-for-profit organizations have grown and have become more corporate in their organizations and management approaches. These organizations are hiring analysts and managers to grow and develop their organizations.

Private Industry

The industrialists, the major polluters and consumers of our natural resources, are under increased public scrutiny to cut pollution at the source—where the products are made. The primary metal, chemical, petroleum, and paper industries are long-standing industries that all need help in revising and rethinking traditional nonenvironmentally sensitive practices.

Education

Educating the masses about the critical need to clean up, monitor, and safeguard our environment is one of the most important environmental careers, because of the changes in behavior it may cause. Teachers at the elementary and high school levels are helping to create an environmental ethic in a new generation of youth. In addition, consultants and trainers will be needed to educate managers and future business leaders at both the college and corporate levels.

Consulting

As a result of new regulations and consumer demand, many companies are seeking help during transition phases when information is needed to educate management. Technical and environmental management experts work directly with businesses on compliance and proactive management policies.

Law

Environmental law is one of the fastest growing areas of legal study today. Lawyers help draft new legislation for improving the environment and help in holding polluters responsible for their actions. Environmental lawyers rely on the expertise of consultants and engineers to help tighten their litigation.

Science

Scientists from chemists to biologists to anthropologists are continually researching and finding out more about the Earth. They assess the type of effects various activities have and propose solutions for conserving the Earth's resources.

Retail

As consumer demand continues to create markets for environmentally sensitive products, new opportunities are being created for new products and packaging. Managers will need to understand the wants and needs of their customers and respond to new legislation that requires more precise terms for labeling and packaging.

Agriculture

New opportunities have developed for those people working in agriculture, due to consumer demand for quality food and con-

tent information. New markets have emerged for organic produce and foods, as concern about pesticides continues to grow. A
number of new jobs have been created for those with expertise in
pest management, organic gardening, retailing organic food, and
on-line and mail-order sales.

Communication
Communicators are needed in both the public and private sectors to explain new policies, highlight the activities of public
interest groups, work on technical journals, and report on environmental events and issues. New positions are being created at
newspapers across the country for the environmental writer, and
the number of environmental magazines and journals continues
to grow.

Finance
Professions that have not traditionally been directly concerned
with environmental issues, such as banking, accounting, and
insurance, are now finding themselves affected by environmental problems. Banks now have to consider the environmental
policies of the companies they lend money to. The growth of
environmental funding and investing in service and cleanup
industries has created new positions in response to consumer
demand for investment opportunities. Insurance companies provide policies to the firms that are at risk for environmental acci-
dents. As a result, environmentally aware underwriters are now
in demand.

Entrepreneurs
The opportunities are endless for the creative, environmentally
aware individual or corporation to create new products and
new businesses in response to consumer demand. From recycling

businesses to environmental cosmetics, the entrepreneur will find a large and receptive market.

Case Study: Energy Star®

Energy Star is a collaboration between the U.S. Department of Energy (DOE), the Environmental Protection Agency (EPA), and the private sector. It is a highly successful government and industry partnership that improves energy efficiency, saves consumers money, creates economic opportunities, and protects the environment.

Since the Energy Star program began in 1992, the EPA and DOE have forged partnerships with more than fifteen hundred companies to bring better, energy efficient products to consumers. More than twelve hundred manufacturing partners now ship more than fifty million Energy Star qualified products each year. Some of these companies include General Electric; Sun Microsystems; Sears, Roebuck and Co.; and Panasonic. By joining the Energy Star program, manufacturers get the opportunity to:

- Increase sales and profits

- Show environmental leadership

- Differentiate their products

- Enhance corporate image

- Gain marketing advantage

If all households and businesses in the United States bought Energy Star qualified products instead of conventional new equipment during the next fifteen years, the national annual energy bill would be reduced by about $100 billion. The reduction in greenhouse gas emissions (carbon dioxide) would be equivalent to taking seventeen million cars off the road for each of those fifteen years.

Inherent in the adoption of Energy Star by the private sector is the creation of many new positions for a diverse group of people with environmental interests. Environmentally literate scientists, manufacturers, engineers, writers, and professionals in public relations, sales, and advertising are just a sampling of the growing careers opportunities made possible by the Energy Star partnership.

Implications for the Workplace

In the process of reorienting the corporate culture to adopt environmental ethics, many established and new businesses will need the services of individuals with an environmental background. As you can see, the opportunities are almost endless for new types of employment in a greener corporate America. The direction your career takes depends on your individual interests and areas of study. While more and more educational institutions are adding environmental components to their existing curriculums, there are still many ways for you to customize your career in the mainstream private sector by adding your own unique environmental interests and values.

Finding Employment in Green-Collar America

Before making a decision about where and how you fit into a greener corporate America, you need to evaluate yourself to understand how to best market yourself in areas of environmental employment. The following is a list of things you need to consider before making a commitment to a specific career.

- *Values*. One of the first issues you will need to examine will be how your environmental values compare to your potential employer's. In addition, because so many areas of the environment need our attention, you will need to decide where you want to focus your efforts. You need to understand and examine how and where your specific skills will be most valuable and useful and how these skills could fit into the overall management of an environmental organization.

- *Goals*. You need to ask yourself what you want to accomplish by working for an environmentally sensitive organization. Are you willing to work diligently and continuously to better our Earth? Are you patient enough to accept each small accomplishment as a very small but important part of the task of cleaning up the destruction of the Industrial Revolution? Are you prepared to fight for what you believe in with powerful private businesses and governments?

- *Skills*. In order to find a job that has an environmental component, you need to bring two types of skills to the position. You will need to be well trained in a technical profession, such as engineering, marketing, or finance, and also be well educated in legal, regulatory, scientific, and political issues as they relate to the environment. To do this, you must study, read, volunteer, and educate yourself in the environmental issues and policies that exist today and those that are being considered for the future.

- *Research and networking*. As you begin your job search you will need to know who is taking the lead in areas that interest you. As a citizen, you have access to corporations' annual reports and 10-K IRS filings that disclose environmental matters and expenditures. Networking just means getting to know people who are already working in environmental careers or organizations. In addition to helping you narrow your area of expertise, the people you meet may be the ones who will help you get a job.

Interviewing for an Environmental Job

The reality of the present job market is that, for many, the environment is a sensitive issue. At this point in time, an environmental philosophy is relatively new to many corporations and you must acknowledge that at least having a philosophy is an improvement. If you are embarking on an environmental career, you must also be willing to work with the polluters to correct decades of unguarded development. Understanding the complexity of instituting new policies and overall change will get you far in your first interview. Some of the guidelines for a successful interview are as follows.

1. Do your homework. Try to understand generally what the company's past policies have been and how they are evolving into greener policies.

2. Demonstrate that you are up-to-date on environmental issues by knowing what environmental claims the company is making through its advertising. Research these claims and think creatively about how the advertising impacted you. Share your perceptions as a consumer with your interviewer.

3. Acknowledge that no company is perfect and understand and show appreciation for progress that has been made.

4. Do not use the interview to bash the company for past environmental policies.

5. Express your desire to participate in future growth and change.

During the interview you will also want to ask about the company's plans for future growth in environmental areas and about plans for adding new positions, divisions, and strategies for environmental management. In conclusion, what you need to bring to the interview is knowledge, ideas, enthusiasm, and an understanding of the major issues facing corporate America in relation to environmental issues.

For More Information

Careers in the Environment 2nd Ed. (2000). By Michael Fasulo and Paul Walker and published by VGM Career Books.

Green at Work (1995). By Susan Cohn and published by Island Press.

CHAPTER FOUR

Careers in Government

T he United States has long been recognized as the world leader in environmental protection and preservation. Our nation has the largest body of professionals and resources directed towards environmental concerns and the toughest antipollution measures in the world. Americans, it is said, are enamored by nature like no other people on Earth. Only baseball surpasses the enjoyment of the great outdoors as a national pastime! Furthermore, citizens look to the government to keep their natural surroundings pristine and themselves safe from environmental hazards.

Environmental issues, especially those linked with health threats, have, in fact, become so prevalent in the last few years that the government now claims the environment to be a top national priority.

U.S. Environmental Policy and Its Effect on Government Jobs

While the environment has only recently resurfaced as a hot political issue, federal involvement in environmental protection and preservation has a long and impressive history. The federal government jumped headlong into creating what is now the most extensive national park and forest system in the world when in 1872 Congress made Yellowstone our first national park.

In the early 1900s, President Teddy Roosevelt, a great out-
doorsman, charted the direction of national environmental policy when he appointed Gifford Pinchot as the Secretary of the
Department of Agriculture. Under Pinchot's stewardship, the
federal government took the lead in developing public lands for
both recreational and industrial use. In 1902, the Department of
Agriculture formed the National Forest Service, and in 1916 the
National Park Service was added to the Department of Interior.
With the addition of many national parks and forests in the
ensuing years, these departments grew, but the driving philosophy behind American environmentalism was one based solely on
resource conservation.

An abrupt broadening of federal environmental policy, fueled
mostly by public concern, took place in the 1960s. In 1962,
Rachel Carson released her now-famous book *Silent Spring*, in
which the great dangers of the pesticide DDT were first exposed.
This work attuned the public to the harms caused by industrial
pollution and is credited with igniting the birth of the age of
modern environmentalism. What resulted in the following years
was a flurry of federal legislative action designed to preserve the
environment and, as importantly, to protect public health.

The result of this legislative activity was the broadening of
federal involvement in all environmental matters. In order for
the federal government to keep up with its new regulatory pow-
ers, a large number of new commissions, committees, and offices
were formed. In addition, the Environmental Protection Agency
was created as an independent agency to act as the nation's environmental nerve center.

Since the early 1980s, the federal government has relegated
much of the enforcement of environmental laws to the states.
Thus, a rippling effect has occurred where the states have also
greatly broadened their environmental protection activities and
workforce. In fact, states like California and New Jersey have
enacted environmental protection laws that far exceed regula-

tions already set by the federal government. As the work of state and local environmental agencies grows there will be a need for a larger and better-trained corps of environmental professionals.

There are thousands of job opportunities at the federal, state, and local levels for people with all different types of employment and educational backgrounds. In sum, the outlook for employment opportunities for the career-minded environmentalist at all levels of government is outstanding.

Pay and Job Benefits for Government Workers

Government employees generally earn lower wages than their counterparts in private industry, but they usually receive better benefits like vacation time, medical plans, flexible work hours, and greater job security. Federal employees receive the highest average pay and are followed, in order, by state, county, and local civil servants. In all levels of government, there are strict hiring and salary regulations. While you will rarely be in a position to negotiate salary or job responsibilities, you can be confident that you'll be treated fairly and equally with all other applicants. The old saying, "It's not what you know but who you know," is much more applicable in the private sector.

In the federal government, the pay schedule, or general schedule (GS), is divided into eighteen pay steps. Within each GS step, there are ten pay levels. The actual pay difference between the lowest and highest levels within each GS step differs by about 30 percent. Table 1 shows the GS pay schedule as of January 2000.

Starting level of pay depends on an applicant's level of education and relative professional experience. In general, you can expect to start at the lowest level of each GS pay step. Those

Table 1. General Schedule Steps and Pay Range

Step	Lowest Pay	Highest Pay
GS-5	$21,370	$27,778
GS-6	$23,820	$30,966
GS-7	$26,470	$34,408
GS-8	$29,315	$38,108
GS-9	$32,380	$42,091
GS-10	$35,658	$46,359
GS-11	$39,178	$50,932

with a high school or equivalent diploma can expect to receive GS-5 wages. A bachelor's degree will earn you a GS-7 rating, while a master's will secure a GS-9 rate. Those who have earned a Ph.D. will be rewarded with the GS-11 pay rate. In order to jump up one full GS step, you must go through a complete annual performance evaluation. Periodic pay raises within each GS step are usually routine. State hiring practices and salaries are structured similarly.

Finding a Federal Government Job

There are literally thousands of jobs openings in the federal government each year for career-minded environmentalists. Only about one-third of these jobs are in Washington, D.C., so, contrary to common belief, you do not have to move to Washington when considering a career in the federal government. There are jobs in federal regional offices in every state and major city and in a large number of counties.

Because of the large number of departments, agencies, and offices in the federal government, you could easily get bogged down in a time-consuming and exhausting search of just a fraction of the jobs that match your interests and/or professional strengths. Many job hunters have likened this job search to an unsolvable maze that has only one entrance and no escape. Figure 1 shows a breakdown of the environmental responsibilities in the major parts of the executive branch of government. This illustration will give you a clearer idea of the types of environmental problems with which each major executive branch deals.

Figure 1. Major Executive Branch Agencies with Environmental Responsibilities

President				
Executive Office of the President				
White House Office	Council on Environmental Quality	Office of Management and Budget		
Overall policy Agency coordination	Environmenal policy Oversight of the National Environmental Policy Act Environmental quality reporting	Budget Agency coordination and management		
Environmental Protection Agency	Department of the Interior	Department of Agriculture	Department of Commerce	Department of State
Air & water pollution Pesticides Radiation Solid waste Superfund Toxic substances	Public lands Energy Minerals National parks	Forestry Soil conservation	Oceanic and atmospheric monitoring and research	International environment
Department of Justice	Department of Defense	Department of Energy	Department of Transportation	Department of Housing and Urban Development
Environmental litigation	Civil works construction Dredge and fill permits Pollution control from defense facilities	Energy policy coordination Petroleum allocation Research and development	Oceanic and atmospheric monitoring and research	International environment
Department of Health and	Department of Labor	Nuclear Regulatory Commission	Tennessee Valley Authority	
Health	Occupational health	Licensing and regulating nuclear power	Electric power generation	

(Human Services)

Source: *Environmental Quality, Sixteenth Annual Report of the Council on Environmental Quality.* Washington, D.C.: U.S. Government Printing Office, 1987.

The next step in the job-hunting process is locating the job openings in the particular agencies in which you're interested. USAJOBS, the federal government's employment information system, provides worldwide job vacancy information, employment information fact sheets, job applications and forms, and has on-line resume development and electronic transmission capabilities. USAJOBS can be accessed via a personal computer, the telephone, or at touch-screen computer kiosks located in Office of Personnel Management offices and many federal buildings nationwide. In addition, the system is available twenty-four hours a day, seven days a week.

You may apply for most jobs with a resume, or the Optional Application for Federal Employment (OF-612), or any written form you choose. For jobs that are filled through automated procedures, such as the Internet, federal agencies may require that you submit a resume and/or other specialized forms. Jobs with unique requirements may also require special forms. For any job you select, it is essential that you follow the instructions for applying that are given in the vacancy announcement and that your application contain the following:

- Job Information—Announcement number

- Personal Information—Full name, mailing address (with zip code), day and evening phone numbers (with area code), social security number, country of citizenship, veterans' preference, and reinstallment eligibility, highest federal civilian grade held, if applicable

- Education—High School name and address, college or university name, and address and type and year of any degrees received (if no degree, show total credits earned)

- Work Experience—Job title, duties and accomplishments, employer's name and address, references, starting and ending dates (month and year), and salary; indicate whether your current supervisor may be contacted.

• Other Qualifications—Job-related training courses (title and year), skills, certificates and licenses, honors, awards, and special accomplishments

You can access USAJOBS at www.usajobs.opm.gov or by looking in your local phone book under the government blue pages for federal buildings or one of the seventeen Personnel Management offices (OPM).

There are also private companies that compile job-listing information and offer these lists in the form of periodicals. The subscription rate for these listings tends to be quite high, but most of these publications are available for you to browse through free of charge at many public and college libraries. The following two publications list a large number of federal job openings.

• *Federal Career Opportunities*. Published by Federal Research Service, Inc., P.O. Box 1059, Vienna, VA 22183. This is a biweekly publication that lists thousands of federal job vacancies. It is organized by general service (GS) series within each agency. It also lists the names of the agency contact people as well as their telephone numbers.

• *Federal Job Digest*. Published biweekly by Breakthrough Publications, Inc. It contains more than three thousand job vacancies in federal agencies throughout the country.

Some other less reputable individuals advertise federal jobs, most notably in newspaper classified ads, offering to land you a government job for a fee. Please keep in mind that there are no fee-based government job announcements; you should never pay for information that is readily available to you for free.

Another excellent way to find out about federal employment is to attend a federal job fair. Job fairs are held throughout the country and are advertised in local newspapers. Call the employment office of any agency to find out when they are holding a job fair. These fairs are organized by either individual agencies or by a group of agencies with similar job openings. Job fairs are often conducted in large arenas or convention halls with scores of agencies and hundreds of job types to choose from. There are information booths where you can speak directly with someone about job openings. In many cases, on-the-spot interviews are conducted and if your credentials are impressive, agencies are often authorized to make an immediate job offer. You should, therefore, approach these fairs just as you would any job interview.

You can also visit your local state Employment Service office. There you will find information on current federal job opportunity listings. The list may be on a printed report, on microfiche, or on computer. The method varies from state to state.

Other good sources of information are Internet job search engines. Many contain listings of government and private-sector job opportunities compiled by the state Employment Service offices throughout the nation.

Additional Sources of Information

Find a Federal Job Fast (1999). By Ronald Krannich and published by Impact Publications. Offers tips on finding government jobs and careers.

The Book of U.S. Government Jobs (2000). By Dennis V. Damp and published by Bookhaven Press. Walks job seekers through the federal hiring process.

A Note on Government Bureaucracy

There are certain advantages and disadvantages to working in government. First, we are all familiar with its reputation as a sluggish and ineffective bureaucracy. One must beware that government agencies tend to foster large, impersonal work atmospheres where one can easily get lost in the bureaucratic shuffle. The career-minded environmentalist should be cautious of dead-end jobs and the "old boy" network that could block your career advancement. In recent years, government agencies have been working hard to dispel their bureaucratic reputations. Management techniques borrowed from the private sector, which bring everyone into the decision-making process and encourage innovative thinking, have been introduced and are working.

Environmental Careers in Major Federal Departments and Agencies

The following is only a partial listing of jobs for environmentalists in the federal government. While there are many other departments, agencies, and offices that hire environmental professionals, these have the heaviest concentrations of environmental jobs and are, therefore, described in detail.

Environmental Protection Agency (EPA)

The EPA was created in 1970 as an independent agency to consolidate the environmental activities of five executive departments and various other agencies. Its basic purpose is to carry out federal laws to protect the environment, especially in the areas of clean air and water. The EPA is responsible for the enforcement of most federal environmental laws, giving the agency a full agenda. The EPA has grown tremendously since its inception and is now the largest regulatory agency in the U.S. government in terms of budget and personnel. In 1970, the EPA employed fifty-four hundred people with an operating budget of $900 million, while today it has nineteen thousand employees and a budget of more than $6 billion! There are six thousand people working at the EPA's headquarters in Washington, D.C., which serves as its administrative center, and there are an additional thirteen thousand environmental professionals employed at the EPA's ten regional offices. These offices are located in Boston, New York, Philadelphia, Atlanta, Chicago, Dallas, Kansas City (Kansas), Denver, San Francisco, and Seattle. The regional offices are responsible for carrying out and enforcing all federal environmental laws and regulations. The regional personnel work directly with state and local agencies, industry, organizations, and individuals.

The EPA is organized into nine divisions that deal with specific environmental areas. These programs include administration and resource management, enforcement and compliance, environmental information, air and radiation, water, pesticides and toxic substances, solid waste, emergency response, international activities, and research and development. In addition there are twenty-five EPA scientific research facilities located throughout the nation.

The EPA hires hundreds of new employees annually—most of these openings are at entry-level positions (GS 5, 7, and 9). A little more than half of all new employees have some type of scientific training. The most frequently advertised job opening is for environmental engineers. The majority of the remaining job openings are for environmental protection specialists. Environmentalists with backgrounds in political science, sociology, geography, economics, community planning, public policy, environmental studies, communication, and journalism are all well represented in these positions. These specialists do a great variety of work, including developing regulations and policy, preparing and reviewing environmental impact statements, handling public relations, and consulting state and local officials. The EPA also offers a wide variety of internships, fellowships, and student programs, most of which are community based and located throughout the country.

The EPA's scope has broadened to include international concerns, such as ozone depletion and global warming, and the agency has developed innovative projects, such as market incentive programs and a greater call for voluntary action from industry to reduce pollution. The EPA does little of the actual research and fieldwork; it primarily administers programs to environmental consultants who carry out the actual work.

Working for the EPA can be a rewarding but at times frustrating experience. It seems that the EPA has far fewer human and financial resources than it does environmental responsibilities. This seems to be the most common complaint echoed by EPA employees. Also, the EPA is being constantly criticized by both industry and environmentalists. This type of no-win pressure has earned EPA employees the reputation of being rather thick-skinned to criticism. Regardless of the challenges and drawbacks, working for the EPA places you squarely at the forefront of national and global work on environmental issues. A career in the EPA is also a good stepping-stone to jobs in the private sector. Many environmental consulting and engineering firms hire former EPA employees. The transition to the private sector often brings with it an increase in salary and a bump up the career ladder into positions with more responsibility and prestige.

For more information, visit the website at www.epa.gov.

U.S. Department of Agriculture (USDA)

This department houses a large number of services that focus on environmental activities. The USDA has more than 105,000 employees, making it the largest employer of environmental professionals in the federal government. The USDA works closely with state agricultural agencies as well as with foreign nations. The USDA has traditionally supported environmental values and is highly respected for environmental conservation practices throughout the world.

The USDA is composed of nineteen agencies whose major functions include agricultural research, food nutrition and consumer services, farm and foreign agricultural services, rural development services, and the management of the national forest system. Three agencies—the U.S. Forest Service; the Agricultural Research Service; and the Cooperative State Research, Education, and Extension Service—offer the greatest environmental career opportunities.

For more information on the activities of the USDA, visit the website at www.usda.gov or contact:

U.S. Department of Agriculture
Fourteenth and Independence Avenue SW
Washington, DC 20250

U.S. Forest Service

The Forest Service manages 191 million acres of public land, mostly in 156 national forests in forty-four states, the Virgin Islands, and Puerto Rico. A guiding principle of the service is its formula for mixed land use between industrial and recreational interests. The service has been criticized, especially in the West, for inadequately managing the clear-cutting of timber by logging companies.

Recently, the service adopted an innovative program for tree harvesting that focuses on maintaining species biodiversity. The ongoing controversies involving the spotted owl and other endangered species in the Northwest have ensured that the Forest Service will be at the center of the battle between environmentalists and lumber interests for quite some time.

The Forest Service employs a wide range of environmentalists, including biologists, foresters, and arborists. Any of these backgrounds combined with experience or a degree in business management is advantageous. Forest rangers, who are responsible for the management of public recreational areas, need both a solid understanding of the physical sciences as well as the ability to interact with the public. The service also employs a number of seasonal summer workers and has a limited number of paid intern programs in the Job Corps and the Senior Community Service Employment Program.

For more information on the U.S. Forest Service, visit any Forest Service Ranger Station or go to www.fs.fed.us.

Agricultural Research Service

This is the research branch of the USDA. Some of its recent activities include research on plant and animal production and protection; problems with the distribution of farm products; human nutritional studies; and air, water, and soil conservation. The Agricultural Research Service has more than eight thousand employees, and a large number of these individuals hold advanced degrees in the agricultural and biological sciences. Most of the service's activities are conducted in cooperation with state agencies. A large share of the research is conducted at state and private universities and at field experimental stations. For more information, go to www.ars.usda.gov.

Cooperative State Research, Education, and Extension Service

This service is the educational arm of the USDA and works with state and local partners to form the national Cooperative Extension System. The Extension Service maintains a small staff in Washington, D.C., that provides leadership in developing educational programs for rural American farmers. In addition, state and local cooperative members hire a number of professionals to administer these programs. The focus is on providing scientific knowledge to improve the quality and yields on rural farms. Current Extension concerns include sustainable agriculture, reviving small farms, food safety and quality, and waste management.

The service hires individuals with backgrounds in the agricultural sciences—agronomy, biology, and animal sciences; agricultural economics; the food sciences; and natural resources. Most Extension professionals have master's or bachelor's degrees with some substantive training and are hired through the individual state land-grant universities (each state has at least one).

For more information, contact your local county extension office (offices are listed under local government in the telephone directory) or land-grant university. Additional information is available on the Internet at www.reeusda.gov, or write to:

Cooperative State Research, Education, and Extension Service
U.S. Department of Agriculture
Washington, DC 20250

U.S. Department of the Interior

The Interior Department has the most far-reaching jurisdiction over national environmental issues. Its responsibilities include the protection and management of more than 436 million acres of public land—about 19 percent of the land area in the United States—the protection and preservation of wildlife, management and conservation of wetlands, and the enforcement of federal surface mining regulations. Each year there are nearly 290 million visitors to the 379 national parks, 36 million visitors to the 530 national wildlife refuges, and 75 million visitors to our public lands.

The Interior Department has five long-term goals: protecting the environment and preserving our nation's natural and cultural resources, providing recreation, managing natural resources, providing scientific research, and servicing Native American tribes and island communities.

The following bureaus fall under the jurisdiction of the Department of Interior: National Park Service; U.S. Fish and Wildlife Service; Bureau of Indian Affairs; Bureau of Land Management; Office of Surface Mining, Reclamation, and Enforcement; Minerals Management Service; U.S. Geological Survey; and Bureau of Reclamation. We will highlight the four bureaus that offer the greatest environmental career opportunities.

For more information, visit the website at www.doi.gov or contact:

U.S. Department of the Interior
1849 C Street, NW
Washington, DC 20240

National Park Service

This service runs the nation's 379 national parks, historic sites, monuments, and recreation areas. Environmental professionals from a wide variety of backgrounds work to formulate and administer National Park Service policies, maintain parklands, and educate the public. Backgrounds in forestry, business administration, geography, parks and recreation, and the physical sciences are well represented in this service. Park rangers, who function as both environmental educators and law enforcement officials, play an important role in the service. There are also many openings for summer seasonal employment. Applications for seasonal employment must be received between September 1 and January 15. For more information, contact the U.S. Department of the Interior for a list of the nine regional National Park Service offices. Each office has specific information on application requirements and available openings for that region. You may also want to contact a park directly for information on current volunteer/permanent positions, or you can go to www.nps.gov.

U.S. Fish and Wildlife Service

This service is responsible for the management of the 530 national wildlife refuges and 150 waterfowl protection areas encompassing more than ninety million acres. Its jurisdiction also includes areas in the national park system that are reserved for hunting and fishing. Its mission is to "preserve and enhance fish and wildlife and their habitats for the continuing benefit of the American people." Other responsibilities include the enforcement of wildlife laws, surveillance of pesticide use, and the listing of endangered species. The service employs professionals with specific training in fields like fish and wildlife biology, wildlife management, limnology, toxicology, and taxonomy, as well as engineering and chemistry.

For more information, visit the website at www.fws.gov.

U.S. Geological Survey (USGS)

The USGS was established in 1879 to provide for "the classification of public lands and the examination of geological structure, mineral resources, and products of the national domain." Its original project was to map the entire nation and make this information available to the public. Its present concerns focus on investigating natural hazards like earthquakes, volcanoes, landslides, floods, and droughts and to examine the nation's mineral and water resources. The USGS is one of the government's most productive services in terms of the number of scientific studies that it publishes. Employees include geographers, cartographers, geologists, engineers, and others trained in the physical sciences.

For more information, visit the website at www.usgs.gov or contact:

U.S. Geological Survey
601 National Center
Reston, VA 20192

Bureau of Land Management (BLM)

The BLM oversees 270 million acres, which makes it the single largest federal manager of public property. Most of this land is located in the West and Alaska. Its central responsibility is to manage energy and mineral exploration by private companies. The bureau maintains a policy of multiple use and sustainable yield practices for its three principal interests: forestry, mining and recreation. Its close ties with industry have earned it the reputation of being pro-development and quite unsympathetic to environmental concerns. The BLM primarily recruits individuals with training in the "hard" sciences, such as civil engineers, mineral and petroleum engineers, cartographers, and biologists. There are also a limited number of openings for social scientists and those with administrative training, primarily in mid- and senior-level positions.

For more information, go to www.blm.gov or contact:

U.S. Bureau of Land Management
Office of Public Affairs
1849 C Street, Room 406-LS
Washington, DC 20240

Bureau of Reclamation

These folks are considered the "busy beavers" of the federal government because they have overseen the construction of most major dam projects in the West. In addition, the bureau provides water to towns, farms, and industry; oversees the generation of hydroelectric power; and provides river regulation and water control measures. The administration of water rights is no small chore because the semiarid West has grown tremendously in population and in acres used for farming and livestock in the last twenty years. The bureau has had a stormy relationship with environmental groups and has fought some historic battles with the Sierra Club over the building of dams such as Hetch Hetchy in Yosemite National Park, Hoover on the Colorado River, and the proposed dam at the head of the Grand Canyon. Thus, the atmosphere at this bureau is often politically charged.

The bureau primarily hires individuals with degrees in civil and mechanical engineering, geology, hydrology, and the soil sciences. For more information, visit the website at www.usbr.gov.

U.S. Department of Commerce

National Oceanic and Atmospheric Administration (NOAA)

This administration's mission is to map, chart, and explore the ocean and to monitor, describe, and predict conditions in the atmosphere and space environment. Americans are very familiar with two of NOAA's activities: it provides the public with daily weather forecasts and advises of any potential destructive natural events through the National Weather Service, and it makes available to the public a complete mapping of all the nation's navigable waterways. Presently, NOAA is assessing the consequences of accidental environmental modification (pollution) and its effects on the Earth and its human population over several scales of time. To their credit, scientists at NOAA (along with NASA) discovered and now monitor the ozone holes over the Arctic and Antarctica. NOAA is also involved in research on alternatives to ocean dumping and in the development of national policies for ocean mining and energy exploration. NOAA is well respected both nationally and internationally for its technical knowledge of environmental problems.

NOAA employs a wide range of professionals with expertise in meteorology, oceanography, cartography, geography, geology, mathematics, and physics.

For more information, visit the website at www.doc.gov or contact:

U.S. Department of Commerce
Fourteenth Street and Constitution Avenue NW
Washington, DC 20230

U.S. Department of Labor

Occupational Safety and Health Administration (OSHA)

OSHA was created in 1970 to enforce all federal safety and health regulations. Its ongoing job is to improve safety standards in the workplace and improve workplace health, to maintain records on job-related injuries and illnesses, and to monitor federal agency safety programs. In fact, it was OSHA that pushed for public disclosure on the dangers of asbestos.

OSHA has a number of openings for safety and occupational health specialists, industrial hygienists, and policy analysts. Filling these positions are career-oriented environmentalists with backgrounds in the health sciences, including occupational health nurses, engineers, and social scientists. For more information, go to www.doi.gov or contact:

U.S. Department of Labor
Office of Public Affairs
200 Constitution Avenue NW, Room S-1032
Washington, DC 20210

U.S. Department of Defense

Army Corps of Engineers

The corps has an unsavory reputation among environmentalists because it has, in the past, vigorously perused engineering projects on rivers, harbors, and waterways without taking into account the environmental damage to aquatic flora and fauna. Twenty years ago it straightened out the meandering Kissimmee River in Florida to control seasonal flooding. This extensive canal and dam system has wreaked such damage to the fragile surrounding wetlands and wildlife that the government will spend millions of dollars over the next several years to restore the river to its original meandering state. The corps is, however, responsible for the enforcement of the regulations pertaining to the nation's wetlands, which is a large and very important task. During the past few years, a battle has been brewing over the definition and designation of wetlands, and the corps is squarely in the middle of this debate.

The corps is a branch of the U.S. Army but hires civilians for all types of engineering positions. For more information, visit the website at www.usace.army.mil or contact:

U.S. Army Corps of Engineers
441 G Street NW
Washington, DC 20314

National Science Foundation (NSF)

The NSF awards grants and scholarships for research and education in all areas of science and engineering. In recent years, an increasing number of awards have been granted to programs and projects geared toward environmental problems. While no actual research is conducted by the NSF, its staff reviews and analyzes research proposals in such areas as engineering, agriculture, science, medicine, education, and public affairs. Thus, the NSF sets the national agenda for exploring scientific knowledge. Staff members work primarily in their areas of interest and gain a solid understanding of the latest research issues.

Since the NSF is involved in such a breadth of scientific issues, it hires individuals with training in both the physical and social sciences. At the purely administrative level, aspiring professionals with degrees in management, accounting, and contract administration are solid candidates.

For more information, go to www.nsf.gov or contact:

National Science Foundation
4201 Wilson Boulevard
Arlington, VA 22230

Congressional Research Service (CRS)

The CRS is the independent and nonpartisan research and reference arm of Congress. Its staff works directly and exclusively with individual member of Congress. Staff members conduct research, analyze policy issues, and answer questions for congressional members. Thus, the CRS is the heart and soul of the information flow through Congress. There are two divisions that deal with environmental issues: Science Policy Research and Environment and Natural Resources.

The service looks for individuals who excel in their academic fields. Many staff positions are for policy analysts with backgrounds in sociology, economics, foreign affairs, biological sciences, engineering, and the physical sciences. Reference librarians and paralegal assistants are also in demand. The CRS also offers a limited number of unpaid volunteer positions for college students.

For more employment information, contact:

Staffing Team
CRS Administrative Office
James Madison Memorial Building, LM 208
The Library of Congress
Washington, DC 20540

Council on Environmental Quality (CEQ)

This council was created to formulate and promote national policies to improve the quality of the environment and report the
findings directly to the president. The council prepares the
Annual Environmental Quality Report for the president,
appraises federal programs to determine if they promote sound
environmental policy, and oversees the implementation of the
National Environmental Policy Act. This office also hires a small
number of researchers with varied college training.

For more information, go to www.whitehouse.gov or contact:

The White House
1600 Pennsylvania Avenue NW
Washington, DC 20500

Peace Corps

The Peace Corps was created to promote world peace and friend-
ship through the helping activities of its volunteers. These volunteers are sent to more than seventy countries throughout the
world to help solve development problems. This work is conducted through the following six program areas: agriculture,
education, health, urban development, small business development, and the environment. This is a wonderful way to learn
new customs, languages, and technical skills, as well as tradi-

tional practices and lifestyles that have a low impact on the environment. Volunteers go abroad for two years and live in the communities in which they work. Some of the benefits include:

- Foreign language training

- All expenses paid during Peace Corps service

- Opportunities for graduate school scholarships and fellowships

- Partial cancellation of eligible Perkins loans and deferment of most federally guaranteed college loans

- Complete medical and dental care during Peace Corps service

- Easier access to federal jobs through noncompetitive eligibility

- $5,400 readjustment allowance after twenty-seven months of service

In addition to volunteer positions, there are jobs for those interested in recruitment and managerial careers. For information on becoming a volunteer, go to www.peacecorps.gov or contact:

Peace Corps
Office of Volunteer Services
Washington, DC 20526

AmeriCorps

AmeriCorps is the domestic Peace Corps. It engages more than forty thousand Americans in community service each year. It is a ten-month, full-time residential service program for men and women ages eighteen to twenty-four. AmeriCorps promotes leadership and team building through its core initiatives: education, public safety, the environment, and other human needs. All members receive health insurance, child care, and a stipend of between $7,400 and $14,800 to cover basic living expenses. After the successful completion of one year of service, members are eligible for an education award of $5,000 per year, up to two years, to apply toward college tuition expenses.

All members live at one of the five AmeriCorps regional campuses—Denver, Colorado; Charleston, South Carolina; San Diego, California; Perry Point, Maryland; and Washington, D.C.—though projects may take members to other communities throughout their region.

For more information, contact an AmeriCorps representative in your home state. You can find state-specific information and application instructions at www.americorps.org.

Environmental Opportunities in Other Federal Departments

There are numerous other places in the federal government for the environmentalist. In the Department of Transportation, try the Federal Aviation Administration, Federal Highway Administration, Materials Transportation Bureau, and the National Transportation Safety Board. At the independent commissions, there are environmental jobs at the Consumer Product Safety Board, Federal Energy Regulatory Commission, Federal Maritime Commission, and the Federal Trade Commission.

Jobs in Congress

There are numerous job opportunities for the career-minded environmentalist on Capitol Hill. The primary reason for this is that there is a 40 percent staff turnover rate per year. The work atmosphere on the "Hill" is much different of that in most other parts of government. The work pace is on the "boom or bust" cycle, with staffers working feverishly for days on end, followed by a few days of calm before the next crisis. Congressional staffers are the true movers and shakers in the halls of Congress, for they do a lion's share of the work and receive little if any of the credit. Career-seeking environmentalists who have a flair for the fast-paced political game and the fortitude to work long hours and receive little pay will find the Hill a rewarding experience. While few staffers stay on the Hill for more than a year or two, the experience and connections made there more than compensate for the drawbacks.

A Brief Tour Through Congress

Congress is made up of the House of Representatives and the Senate. Each state has two senators, while the number of representatives varies by state population. Vermont, for example, has one congressperson while California has more than forty. Staff workers in Congress are not federal employees, and Congress has exempted itself from most federal hiring and salary regulations. Thus, the job search process in Congress is more like that of the private sector because there are few if any bureaucratic procedures for congressional offices to follow.

Each senator and representative maintains two sets of staff: one in the home district and one in Washington, D.C. The Washington offices have the larger and more politically active staff. You should concentrate your search on congressional members who have reputations as environmentalists (most of these are Democrats). Other members of Congress are deeply involved in environmental issues through their work on the twenty-five committees in both the House and Senate that have an environmental agenda. Figure 2 is a list of the committees and subcommittees that focus on these environmental issues.

Figure 2. Congressional Committees and Their Jurisdictions

The following are the congressional committees with jurisdiction over environmentally related programs and the programs for which each committee is responsible.

SENATE

Agriculture
Soil conservation, groundwater
Forestry, private forest reserves
Pesticides, food safety
Global change

Appropriations
International monetary and financial funds
Forest Service
Army Corps of Engineers
Nuclear Regulatory Commission
Tennessee Valley Authority
Occupational Safety and Health Administration (OSHA)
Mine Safety and Health Administration
Soil conservation programs
Food and Drug Administration
Environmental Protection Agency
Council on Environmental Policy
National Oceanic and Atmospheric Administration

Armed Services
Military weapons plants
Nuclear energy
Naval petroleum, oil shale reserves
Air Force jet emissions

Commerce, Science, Transportation
Coastal zone management
Inland waterways
Marine fisheries
Oceans, weather, science research
Outer continental shelf
Global change

Energy and Natural Resources
Energy policy, conservation
National parks, wilderness
Nuclear energy, public utilities
Public lands, forests
Global change

Environment and Public Works
Environmental policy, oversight
Air and water pollution
Outer continental shelf
Toxic substances
Fisheries and wildlife
Flood control, deepwater ports
Ocean dumping
Nuclear energy
Bridges, dams, inland waterways
Solid-waste disposal
Superfund, hazardous waste
Global change

Finance
Revenue measures, user fees
Foreign Relations
Nuclear energy, international
International Monetary Fund
International environmental affairs

(Figure 2 continued)

Government Affairs
Nuclear export policy
Nuclear weapons plant cleanup

Judiciary
Environmental law, penalties

Labor and Human Resources
Occupational health and safety
Pesticides, food safety

HOUSE

Agriculture
Agriculture and industrial chemistry
Soil conservation, groundwater
Forestry and private forest reserves
Pesticides, food safety
Global change

Appropriations
International monetary funds
Forest Service
Army Corps of Engineers
Nuclear Regulatory Commission
Tennessee Valley Authority
Occupational Safety and Health Administration (OSHA)
Mine Safety and Health Administration
Soil conservation programs
Food and Drug Administration
Environmental Protection Agency
Council on Environmental Policy
National Oceanic and Atmospheric Administration

Armed Services
Military weapons plants
Naval petroleum, oil shale reserves
Nuclear energy

Banking, Finance, and Urban Affairs
International financial and monetary organizations

Education and Labor
Occupational health and safety

Energy and Commerce
Energy policy, oversight
Energy conservation
Health and the environment
Interstate energy compacts
Public health and quarantine
Nuclear facilities
Transportation of hazardous materials
Solid-, hazardous-waste disposal

Foreign Affairs
Foreign loans, International Monetary Fund
International environmental affairs
Global change

Government Operations
Environment, energy, natural resources oversight

Interior and Insular Affairs
Forest reserves (public domain)
Public lands
Irrigation and reclamation

(Figure 2 continued)
Petroleum conservation (public lands)
Conservation of radium supply
Nuclear energy industry

Judiciary
Environmental law, penalties

Merchant Marine and Fisheries
Coastal zone management
Fisheries and wildlife
Oil-spill liability
Wetlands

Public Works and Transportation
Flood control, rivers, and harbors
Pollution of navigable waters
Bridges and dams
Superfund, hazardous waste

Science, Space, and Technology
Research and development
National Weather Service
Global change
Nuclear energy, facilities
Agriculture research
National Oceanic and Atmospheric Administration

Ways and Means
Revenue measures, user fees
Superfund

Source: Phillip Marwill, *Congressional Quarterly Weekly Report*, January 20, 1990, 151.

Committee staff members do not work for specific congressional members but instead work for a committee that deals with specific pieces of environmental legislation. Contact the congressional committees directly for job openings.

Sources of Information

The Almanac of American Politics (annual). By Michael Barone and Grant Ujifusa and published by the National Journal Group. This book gives a full profile on individual members of Congress, their voting records, and how they are rated on such issues as the environment, defense, and economic policy. It is touted as being one of the six books that Jimmy Carter displayed prominently on his White House desk.

The Congressional Staff Directory (annual). Published by CQ Staff Directories. This book lists the names of every congressional staffer, as well as specific biographical information, such as their academic and employment histories and memberships in organizations.

Environmental Careers in State Government

During the past couple of decades, state governments have assumed a major role in developing environmental policies and regulations. California is frequently cited as the state leader in pollution abatement measures, and it appears that other states are also beginning to realize that they need to aggressively address their own environmental problems. Serious issues such as air pollution, urban sprawl, hazardous waste disposal, and drinking water contamination have forced the states to take actions that in many cases go beyond regulations set by the federal government.

State environmental agencies expend most of their energy carrying out specific programs and distributing information, funding, and resources to county and local governments. While the states do not have the number or breadth of environmental departments and agencies that the federal government has, they do offer a wide variety of job opportunities for the career-seeking environmentalist. Also, state environmental specialists are more apt to work on projects from "cradle to grave" and have more input than their federal counterparts. While resources may be more limited at the state level (some states are much more limited than others), these agencies are smaller and tend to be less bureaucratic.

While the number and types of jobs vary widely, each state has its own environmental protection department. This is a good place to start when researching career opportunities. The Appendix provides a list of state environmental protection agencies.

Environmental Careers in Local Government

In local government, the environmentalist will find a potpourri of jobs. The most common denominator for these jobs is the emphasis on hands-on work. A good chunk of the money that federal and state governments allocate for environmental projects is carried out by city, county, and municiple authorities. Water and waste treatment plants, landfills, garbage collection, and recycling programs are some of the projects that local governments operate and/or regulate. These are essential services, and they must be continuously maintained and upgraded.

While federal and state environmental agencies have passed a larger share of responsibility onto local governments in recent years, an increasing number of citizen groups have also been pressuring for better monitoring of community problems. The combination of these demands has made local authorities more responsive to community needs.

Working at the local level is a great way to begin an environmental career. There is a high turnover rate, which translates into a steady flow of job openings. Jobs tend to be oriented toward field operations like program management, inspections, and enforcement, which are the building-block skills that every career-directed environmentalist should learn. Also, the work tends to be decentralized, and new employees are quickly given responsibilities and opportunities to learn valuable leadership skills. Since most work is carried out in small communities or urban neighborhoods, professionals constantly interact with citizens and feel much less a part of the government bureaucracy. There are some drawbacks, such as relatively low pay compared to other government workers and a much greater degree of petty politics, but these jobs often provide a conduit to environmental careers in other parts of government and the private sector.

To find out about these jobs, contact local agencies directly. Look in the local phone book to find the department headings. Many public works and park and recreation departments offer summer jobs to high school and college students. Also, ask neighbors or friends who may know someone employed in one of these departments or a local politician who may be able to pull a few strings.

CHAPTER FIVE

Careers for Eco-Entrepreneurs

New Opportunities for the Eco-Entrepreneur

Many new and wonderful opportunities for the individual with an entrepreneurial spirit have developed as a result of the consumer's increased concern and awareness about the environment. A large and growing market has emerged for products that have been developed, packaged, and marketed with the least possible amount of harm being done to our natural resources, our health, the health of the workers, and the ozone layer. In addition, a new business ethic that has a respect for the environment at its foundation has emerged and is continuing to develop. In Chapter 3, we discussed how traditional jobs are now evolving to include an environmental component. In this chapter, we are discussing new opportunities for businesses that have been conceptualized and developed with environmental concerns in mind.

The desire to own a business, to make money, and to provide useful goods and services no longer is in conflict with good environmental policies. Past realities and misconceptions that green products and services were too expensive for widespread use are diminishing as more and more research and development is done. New, cheaper technologies and large-scale production capabilities are helping to make environmentally sensitive products less expensive and more accessible to the masses.

Another important result of the increased demand for green products is that the gap has begun to close between the grassroots environmentalist (and all the stereotypes that label carries with it) and the business world (and all the stereotypes it carries). Environmentalists have become more business minded and businesses have become more environmentally minded. This trend will continue as our concern for the environment grows, and it eventually will become the norm rather than the exception to the rule.

The opportunities are endless for the entrepreneur. A commitment to the environment coupled with a good idea are two of the essential components for beginning your career as an eco-entrepreneur. In the following pages, we will provide an overview of some of the necessary qualifications for starting your own business and then outline the areas where the opportunities are presently the greatest for the entrepreneur.

What Does It Take to Start Your Own Environmental Business?

Starting your own environmental business requires a lot of hard work and a commitment to blend the desire to make a profit with a strong sense of social responsibility. Consumers today are choosing products that make claims of being environmentally safe over those that do not. Very often these products cost more and sometimes are less convenient (bottles need to be saved, returned, recycled, and refilled) than the modern-day consumer is used to. In order to successfully launch an environmental business or product, a mission statement or overall philosophy of the company needs to be articulated and presented to the buying public.

As you begin formulating the plan for your business, you need to think about the company's philosophy, write it down, and develop it so that it can be expanded and adapted for every area of your business—from product development to in-house environmental policies. As more and more companies make claims about the "greenness" of their products and services, consumers are beginning to demand real information on the quality of the products and commitment of the companies that produce them.

Qualifications

Three areas in which you will need to have well-articulated plans and policies are environmental ethics, recycling programs, and research and development. Clearly defining your goals and commitment in these areas will give you the foundation you need to develop a successful plan for your business. The type and size of your business will help you formulate the philosophy of the organization. However, all of your environmental policies and plans should be flexible enough to grow and adapt with the growth of your business.

Environmental Ethics

A clearly defined commitment to environmental issues and to the protection of our natural resources is one of the most important criteria for consumers in choosing an environmentally safe product over one that is not. An international reliance on rural cultures for raw materials requires that the ethic of the company be one of mutual respect for and investment in social programs in the countries and communities that are providing you with the raw materials to produce your product.

This commitment begins early and could be as simple as donating a certain amount of your profits to social programs or environmental organizations. As the company grows, it should follow that the company's involvement and commitment to social programs also increases. In addition, providing your employees with an environmental work ethic will guarantee that the entire organization is dedicated to providing useful goods and services that have the good of the Earth in mind.

Recycling Programs

An important measure for monitoring a company's commitment to operating its businesses in an environmental manner is how trash is dealt with. This includes in-house policies for recycling and packaging the products you produce. An important question to address is what happens to product containers and packaging when consumers are finished with them? Plans need to be made from the start to use minimal and recyclable packaging, and systems need to be set up to make it as easy as possible for the customer to return, refill, and recycle packaging.

Research and Development Contributions

Consumers are also interested in knowing about how much effort companies are investing in research and development of new products that further promote the protection of our natural resources. Many companies have their own labs that work continually to develop and test new products that don't exploit our natural resources and that are renewable. Consumers are interested in knowing just how committed you are to continued investment in products designed to save the Earth.

Market Environment

In order to start a successful business, it is important to have more than just a good idea or a nice product. Before launching and developing a new product, you need to identify your market and do research to find out if consumers share your desire to invest in the future of the planet.

The amount and type of research you do will depend on the size and scope of your business. The simplest way to investigate how receptive the market will be to your product is to examine your own consumer behavior and that of your friends. Spend time in stores that are promoting environmental products and read magazines, books, and anything else that focuses on environmental concerns.

If the product or service you are planning to start is larger than a basement operation and if you have the resources to hire market researchers to help you define and understand your market, you should do so. Talking and listening to your potential consumers are also essential to get a feel for the issues you will face and the concerns you will encounter.

Financing

Financing a new business—environmental or not—is a key element to the success of any new business venture. Before launching a new business, it will be necessary to investigate the ways to finance your efforts.

Traditional banks are now seriously considering the long-term benefits of investing in environmentally sound companies and, as a result, are much more receptive to investing in companies that have the preservation of our natural resources as a fundamental tenet of the corporate philosophy.

When applying for a loan, investigate which banks have already invested in environmental companies and talk to other eco-entrepreneurs to get information on where they turned to get financial support.

Overview of Entrepreneurial Opportunities

The following is a list of areas where opportunities are plentiful for the eco-entrepreneur. The categories outlined are broad, and many different types of businesses could fall into each category. This list should give you an idea of where the opportunities lie as you begin thinking about your own business plans.

Renewable Energy

Increased public concern about diminishing and expensive resources that provide us with heat, fuel, and the comforts of our day-to-day lives has resulted in a new interest in renewable energies. People with ideas and inventions that promote the use of solar, wind, and other renewable energy sources are becoming more and more in demand. From electric cars to solar homes to rechargeable batteries, the opportunities here are almost limitless.

Recycling

As recycling becomes more and more a part of our everyday lives, new opportunities are emerging. The development of environmentally safe packaging alternatives and the collection and redevelopment of existing materials are two areas where ambitious entrepreneurs can make a difference and a living.

Retail

In response to increased concern about the environment and personal health and well-being, traditional markets that have not taken the environment into consideration are now being forced to do so. From cosmetics to clothing to cleaning products, new markets are emerging for environmentally sensitive products. The naturalness and simplicity of these products hold a great deal of appeal for the consumer who has a heightened awareness of the precarious state of our Earth. Many mail-order businesses have emerged, offering products that have not yet reached the shelves of our department stores. Canvas bags, recycling bins, and 100 percent cotton clothing are just a few of the items now being promoted and sold by eco-entrepreneurs.

Agriculture

A natural outgrowth of the environmental movement is an increased demand by consumers for foods that are preservative and pesticide free. New opportunities have emerged for producers of organic produce and healthy foods. In addition, products developed from renewable natural resources are being well received in the marketplace.

Construction

An integral part of the recycling movement is in the areas of construction and architecture. New buildings and furniture are more commonly being built from existing, used raw materials.

The opportunities here are endless and the financial rewards substantial.

Inventions

Working with existing, ineffective technologies to produce new methods and tools for producing and recycling products is a fast-growing area for the environmental entrepreneur. In addition, new products are being developed with the ultimate goal of replacing existing products with new environmentally sensitive products. A good example of this is in the auto industry, where an increased amount of time and money is being put into the development of electric cars.

Creative Careers

Many other opportunities exist for creative types who carry out their work with the environment in mind. Artists are using recycled materials in their artwork, and writers are writing books on the environment. People are selling goods that they have developed to meet their own needs, and good environmental products are selling.

As you can see, opportunities for the entrepreneur are plentiful. Each of these categories has within it profiles of a diverse group of people with varying skills and educational backgrounds. Some of these entrepreneurial ventures require a great deal of technical expertise, and some just require a commitment to the environment and a good idea. If you choose to pursue a career as an entrepreneur, it will be important for you to think carefully about your own skills and interests and to combine them to develop a business that will be uniquely your own.

As with many other careers outlined in this book, this type of career requires that you possess many skills. Communication skills, an in-depth knowledge of environmental issues, and business training will help make your business a success.

The Eco-Entrepreneurial Network

Integral to the success of your business will be how well you tap into the emerging network and resources available to people like yourself. Magazines, conventions, and organizations exist specifically for environmental entrepreneurs and will be extremely helpful to you as you develop, plan, and launch your own business.

Publications

The following is a brief list of some of the resources available to the eco-entrepreneur. This list is in no way complete, but these publications, in addition to providing you with helpful information, will lead you to additional resources.

In Business: The Magazine for Sustainable Enterprises &
   Communities
JG Press, Inc.
419 State Avenue
Emmaus, PA 18049

Business Ethics Magazine
1107 Hazeltine Boulevard, Suite 530
Chaska, MN 55318

Business as Usual (2001). By Anita Roddick (the Body Shop) and published by Thorsons.

SustainableBusiness.com is an organization with a website that provides lists of "Green Dream Jobs" as well as news updates about environmental developments in the world of business.

Conventions

In response to the increased number of businesses that focus on environmentally safe products, the number of conferences, expos, and meetings has increased. Your best source for finding out about these events is by reading and subscribing to environmental publications. The National Marketplace for the Environment sponsors the annual ECO EXPO with more than four hundred exhibitors. For information about dates and locations, go to the organization's website at www.ecoexpo.com.

Networking

Your most valuable resource, as with any career path you choose to pursue, is yourself and others who are doing similar work. Networking will be an integral part of your success in any career you choose to pursue, but it will be especially helpful if you are choosing to start a business. Eco-entrepreneurs are interested in the successful development of companies like their own and are usually very willing to give advice and information to help you get off to the right start and avoid making the same mistakes they may have made.

CHAPTER SIX

Careers in Nonprofit Organizations

T he great American spirit of altruism is shining as we enter the twenty-first century. Of the many challenges that confront our nation and the world, none is more pressing than the preservation of our fragile environment, and no people have risen to the challenge better than concerned Americans. Since the early 1980s, participation in the environmental movement has soared. Membership in most national environmental groups such as the Sierra Club and the National Audubon Society has doubled or tripled, and thousands of new grassroots (local) environmental organizations have sprung up. The maxim "think globally, act locally" is flourishing as communities around the United States are fighting and winning battles against toxic dumping and pollution and are working together for the health of their families and fellow citizens. Americans are feeling a renewed sense of political and social empowerment, and they are channeling this into environmental activities. The goal is to do something positive for our future, the future of the children, and the future of the Earth upon which we all vitally depend.

This chapter describes opportunities in national, state, and local nonprofit environmental organizations. Of all the job sectors discussed in this book, this is actually the area with the fewest job opportunities. Although the number of new organizations and the level of membership and donations for existing organizations have grown tremendously, only the very largest have professional staffs of more than fifty people, while the majority of organizations have perhaps a handful of paid staff members or all volunteers with no paid staff at all. These organizations are perpetually short of money and are often locked in legal and policy battles with large corporations that have far superior financial and human resources. Add all of this to the fact that the nonprofit sector lags behind both government and the private sector in wages, benefits, and job security.

So, given these facts, why would anyone be interested in pursuing a career with a nonprofit environmental organization? The answer, oddly enough, is quite simple: these people know that they are making a measurable difference in our world through their environmental work. They are working in an exciting and challenging atmosphere that gives them the opportunity to meet hundreds or even thousands of like-minded and highly motivated individuals. In no other job sector are workers more dedicated or determined; many of these individuals view themselves as the fictional David battling the powerful Goliath, and they relish the opportunity to lay the big bully down to defeat!

The Nonprofit World

There are many rich opportunities and ways in which you can do something positive for the Earth by working with nonprofit environmental organizations. In this chapter, you will learn about the nine largest organizations, what they do, and how they operate, and about volunteer and intern positions within these groups. Keep in mind that state and local organizations work with or receive information and funding from these national groups; therefore, these organizations are good contacts for getting information on career opportunities in and around your community. We will also explore regional environmental centers that have listings of volunteer opportunities, internships, and job openings.

In addition, you will learn about two environmental job placement organizations that specialize in finding jobs for career-oriented environmentalists and about additional resources that will help your career search.

Sources of Information

World Directory of Environmental Organizations (2001). By the California Institute of Public Affairs and published by the Sierra Club.

World Environmental Directory (annual). Published by Business Publishers, Inc. Includes thirteen entries with thirty thousand listings of conservation and environmental organizations, pollution-control product manufacturers and consultants, federal and state governments, attorneys with environmental interests, environmental education programs, databases, and funding sources.

National Environmental Organizations

Among these are some well-known organizations, such as the Sierra Club and the National Wildlife Federation. Most of these organizations make their headquarters in Washington, D.C., and have regional offices and/or local chapters throughout the country. These nonprofits serve a duel purpose: they encourage citizen participation at the local level, and they work to influence politicians and create environmental laws at the national level. Since the early 1980s, when membership and funding for many of the established environmental nonprofits soared, they have been showing themselves as a strong political voice in Washington.

There are far more intern and volunteer opportunities than staff positions at most of these organizations, and the best way to land a job is to first do volunteer or intern work. In fact, most jobs openings are not even advertised because they are given directly to interns and volunteers. By donating your time, you will get a firsthand opportunity to see how these organizations operate and can decide if a career in the nonprofit sector is for you. In many cases, intern and volunteer staff will try to match your interests and skills with projects, but be prepared for a good amount of busywork like envelope stuffing and filing.

The type of personnel hired depends largely on the organization and the issues that they pursue, although some generalizations are possible. Good communication and writing skills are essential. Most of these organizations are advocacy groups and, therefore, depend upon their employees to maintain open channels of communication with the public. Among the types of professionals hired are conservation specialists, journalists, policy researchers, economists, lawyers, and health specialists. Also, a good number of the national headquarter staff are administrators and fund-raisers. Individuals with backgrounds in management, finance, and accounting, as well as individuals with fund-raising experience and secretarial skills, are always in demand. The following is a list of some of the largest nonprofit environmental organizations in the country. Also listed are the numbers of supporters and staff members for each organization.

Leading Nonprofit Environmental Organizations in the United States

Organization/ Address	Staff	Members/ Supporters
Environmental Defense Fund 257 Park Avenue South New York, NY 10010	170	300,000

Organization/ Address	Staff	Members/ Supporters
Greenpeace USA 702 H Street NW Washington, DC 20001	250	2,500,000
National Audubon Society 700 Broadway New York, NY 10023	300	550,000
Natural Resources Defense Council 40 West Twentieth Street New York, NY 10011	220	400,000
National Wildlife Federation 1400 Sixteenth Street NW Washington, DC 20036	650	5,000,000
Nature Conservancy 4245 North Fairfax Drive Arlington, VA 22203	2,700	1,000,000
Sierra Club 85 Second Street San Francisco, CA 94105	340	600,000
Wilderness Society 1615 M Street NW Washington, DC 20036	135	317,000
World Wildlife Fund–U.S. 1250 Twenty-fourth Street NW Washington, DC 20037	325	1,000,000

Environmental Defense Fund (EDF)

The Environmental Defense Fund is an organization of lawyers, engineers, scientists, and economists working to improve the state of the environment and to protect public health. The EDF has identified eight areas on which to focus its concern:

- toxic waste

- energy

- acid rain

- wildlife conservation

- global warming

- ozone depletion

- biotechnology

- water resources

In recent years, the EDF has become a leading advocate of economic incentives as a new approach to solving environmental problems. They also publish a large number of reports each year on a variety of environmental issues. Through sustained legal pressure, backed by solid expertise on environmental issues, the EDF has earned a reputation as a tough and effective voice in the environmental arena.

The EDF makes its headquarters in New York City and has five regional offices in Washington, D.C.; Oakland, California; Boulder, Colorado; Raleigh, North Carolina; and Austin, Texas. There are presently 170 staff members nationwide. In addition to support staff, the EDF hires a number of lawyers, conservation scientists, engineers, lobbyists, economists, publicists, and policy analysts. The EDF offers paid internships at each of its offices. Interns are typically upper-level college undergraduates or graduate students and work on issues such as global climate change, recycling, fund-raising, and education. In some cases, students can earn college credit for their work. In order to apply for an internship, send a resume, writing sample, transcript, and a letter describing why you would like to work for the EDF to its national headquarters.

For more information, visit the organization's website at www.edf.org.

Greenpeace USA

Greenpeace is a highly successful nonviolent, direct-action organization dedicated to positive environmental change. It started more than thirty years ago as a small band of concerned environmentalists protesting nuclear testing and has evolved into a huge international grassroots-based organization with offices in more than twenty-five countries and a research station in Antarctica. Its U.S. delegation is headquartered in Washington, D.C., and it has regional offices in large cities like Chicago, San Francisco, Miami, New York, Boston, and Seattle. At present, Greenpeace is focusing its attention on halting the threat of toxic pollutants; protecting endangered species such as whales, dolphins, and seals; and fighting to halt global warming and depletion of the ozone layer.

Greenpeace has more than 250 staff members in the United States working at the main and regional offices. These individuals are involved primarily with fund-raising and grassroots organizing. The organization strongly encourages the inclusion of people of color. In addition, Greenpeace has on its staff a group of conservation specialists, photographers, and professional nature lovers to carry out and publicize the organization's campaigns. Greenpeace has a large group of paid canvassers who conduct door-to-door donation drives. There are also many volunteer opportunities within the organization. Greenpeace encourages grassroots action by its supporters and provides assistance to hundreds of local causes.

For more information, contact the headquarters office or visit the website at www.greenpeace.org.

National Audubon Society (NAS)

The National Audubon Society is a group of citizen and professional conservationists whose goal is to save wildlife and their habitats. While this group has in the past been concerned primarily with the protection of birds and their habitats, the NAS has broadened its concerns to include the conservation of land and water, pollution issues, energy policy, and global environmental concerns. The NAS works toward these goals through activities such as lobbying, litigation, scientific research, sanctuary management, education programs, publications, and film documentaries. The Audubon Adventure Club sponsors educational programs for more than five hundred thousand elementary school children in fourteen thousand classrooms every year.

The National Audubon Society has about three hundred employees working at its headquarters in New York City and its nine regional offices in Anchorage, Alaska; Columbus, Ohio, Camp Hill, Pennsylvania; Albany, New York; Boulder, Colorado; Tallahassee, Florida; Austin, Texas; Manhattan, Kansas; and Sacramento, California. There are also a number of part-time and seasonal employment opportunities. The NAS also offers seasonal paid internships, including a legal intern program in Washington, D.C., and field intern opportunities at Audubon sanctuaries nationwide, where interns learn valuable conservation and teaching skills. For information on internships, contact the Human Resources Department in New York or look into the many volunteer opportunities at Audubon membership chapters and sanctuaries in your area.

For more information, contact the New York office or visit the website at www.audubon.org.

Natural Resources Defense Council (NRDC)

The Natural Resources Defense Council was formed by a group of Yale Law School classmates in 1970. It fights for environmental justice in the courts of law. The NRDC has described its mission and approach to environmental problems as follows: "The power of the law. The power of science. The power of the people. In defense of the environment."

The NRDC is presently involved in a number of issues, including global warming, air and water pollution, energy policy, the preservation of coastal environments, and the protection of rain forests. Its staff, in addition to a corps of lawyers, includes conservation scientists, research specialists, and staff assistants. In addition, the organization publishes the monthly *Amicus Journal*, which is a wonderful source of environmental news and information.

The NRDC maintains a staff of 220 at its national headquarters in New York and at three regional offices in Washington, D.C., Los Angeles, and San Francisco. There is a paid summer intern legal program in New York, as well as a limited number of general internships at each office.

For information on internships and volunteer opportunities, contact the director of volunteers in New York. For employment information, write to the headquarters office or go to the website at www.nrdc.org.

National Wildlife Federation (NWF)

The NWF, which was created under the leadership of Franklin D. Roosevelt in 1936, is involved with conservation efforts in the United States and throughout the world. In terms of membership, the NWF is the largest nonprofit environmental organization in the United States, with more than five million members. The organization's primary goal is to promote the wise use of natural resources through education programs, publications, and research.

The NWF sponsors an annual education program called National Wildlife Week, produces science and social studies curricula for primary and secondary schools, and publishes the annual *Conservation Directory*, which is the listing of who's who in the American conservation movement.

The NWF has 650 paid staff members in its Vienna, Virginia, headquarters and eleven national field offices. The Washington office is concerned mainly with research, fund-raising, lobbying, outreach to other environmental organizations, and research activities. There are independent NWF affiliates located in every state that are concerned with local grassroots activities. These independent affiliates each maintain a small staff and actively recruit volunteers, sponsor activities and outings, and offer a limited number of internships.

The NWF also sponsors the Resource Conservation Alliance, which is a grassroots network of members and a great source of activist information.

For information about the NWF affiliate in your area, contact the Washington office, consult the *Conservation Directory*, or visit the website at www.nwf.org.

Nature Conservancy

The Nature Conservancy is an organization whose aim is to "find, protect, and maintain the Earth's rare species and natural communities by preserving the lands they need to survive." To achieve this goal, the Nature Conservancy locates ecologically sensitive or threatened lands, acquires these lands, and then maintains them as nature preserves.

Presently, the Nature Conservancy manages nearly sixteen hundred preserves on more than eleven million acres of land throughout the United States and more than fifty-five million acres internationally. The organization has entered agreements with other nonprofit organizations and the U.S. government to greatly expand these holdings during the next decade. The Latin America debt-for-nature swap, where governments are forgiven a part of their foreign debts in exchange for creating national nature preserves, is among the Nature Conservancy's great achievements.

The Nature Conservancy's headquarters is in Arlington, Virginia, just outside of Washington, D.C. There are also four regional offices in Boston, Massachusetts; Minneapolis, Minnesota; Chapel Hill, North Carolina; and Boulder, Colorado, as well as local offices in every state. There are presently about twenty-seven hundred professionals working for the Nature Conservancy, which makes it the largest nonprofit environmental employer. Most of these individuals work on the nature preserves and have degrees or experience in resource and wildlife management.

Volunteers are an integral part of the organization's success and are encouraged to take an active role in managing and maintaining the preserves and helping at the local offices. Contact the main or regional offices for the location of the local office or nature preserve nearest to you. Or visit the Nature Conservancy's website at www.nature.org.

Sierra Club

The Sierra Club is one of the oldest, most respected and active environmental organizations in the United States. With chapters in almost every state and four hundred local groups, the Sierra Club is likely to have an office somewhere near you.

At present, the Sierra Club's primary activities include working for clean air and water, designating more protected areas of wilderness in national parks and forests, fighting against global warming and acid rain, and promoting environmental education programs.

There are 340 paid staff positions in the Sierra Club. While a number of jobs are at the Sierra Club's headquarters in San Francisco, California, there are employment opportunities at every chapter. The San Francisco office acts as the information nerve center of the club's activities. The Sierra Club maintains a philosophy of local activism, and the chapters maintain a high level of autonomy from the national headquarters and concentrate mostly on local issues.

In every chapter, volunteers play a key role. With more than four hundred volunteer groups located throughout the United States, members participate in lobbying, letter writing, and organizing campaigns. In addition, the Sierra Club promotes member interest in wilderness experiences and sponsors many backpacking, canoeing, skiing, and bicycling trips. Thus, staff, volunteers, and members have the opportunity to share their experiences and concerns.

For more information, contact the San Francisco headquarters office or visit the website at www.sierraclub.org.

Wilderness Society

The Wilderness Society is devoted to the preservation of wildlife and the wilderness; it concentrates these efforts in government-protected lands such as state and national forests, parks, deserts, rivers, and shore lands. The Wilderness Society works to persuade the government to designate more public land as wilderness areas, which are off limits to any type of development or alteration.

The organization is also conducting an intensive legislative campaign in Congress aimed at reducing the level of funding for road building in national forests, reducing the amount of logging on federal lands, and preserving ancient forests. In conjunction with this project is a study to track the transition of jobs in logging communities so that economic hardships in these communities can be averted.

The Wilderness Society maintains its headquarters in Washington, D.C., and has eight field offices located throughout the United States. The Society has a staff of 135 environmental professionals working in five areas: membership development, finance, administration, resource and economic planning, and conservation. There is also a congressional lobbying staff in Washington, and most of these individuals have previous experience working on Capitol Hill. There are volunteer and unpaid intern opportunities at each office. Inquiries should be made to the main office. On the Internet, visit the organization's website at www.wilderness.org.

World Wildlife Fund (WWF)

The World Wildlife Fund is an international conservation organization dedicated to protecting endangered wildlife and wildlands. The WWF is an affiliate of the international World Wide Fund for Nature network and is one of twenty-four worldwide organizations. The WWF has developed a list of nine goals:

- protect individual species

- protect habitat

- influence public opinion and the policies of governments and private institutions

- support scientific investigation

- promote education in foreign countries

- offer training to local wildlife professionals

- encourage self-sufficiency in developing nations

- monitor international wildlife trade

- promote ecologically sound development

At present, a large share of its funding is being used in Latin America, where the WWF has helped create and now monitors a number of national parks and wildlife reserves.

The WWF employs 325 environmental professionals at its United States office in Washington, D.C. The Washington office is primarily involved with fund-raising, research activities and managing field activities.

A large number of WWF's professional employees have advanced training in the conservation sciences and work at the various field stations throughout the world. There are a limited number of summer internships and one-year research fellowships available. At present, there are no organized volunteer activities in the United States.

For more information, contact the D.C. headquarters or visit the organization's website at www.worldwildlife.org.

Direct Action Organizations

There are other, less formal organizations that prefer the use of direct action tactics over the more traditional methods of negotiation and concession making used by most of the larger environmental organizations. These groups take polluters and those who they consider "environmental criminals" head-on and have used media and public attention very effectively in achieving their goals.

Earth First!

Earth First! uses militant-style tactics to stop logging in the Pacific Northwest, to greatly expand the acreage of designated wilderness areas, and to protect endangered species such as the grizzly and northern timber wolf. The central theme of Earth First! is that there is absolutely "no compromise in the defense of Mother Nature!" Members use tactics such as chaining themselves to trees to block bulldozers and clear-cutting, cutting power lines, and spiking trees to stop environmental destruction.

There are chapters of Earth First! throughout the country, and you can obtain a list of contacts by visiting the website at www.earthfirstjournal.org or writing:

The Earth First! Journal
P.O. Box 1415
Eugene, OR 97440

Sea Shepherd Conservancy

The Sea Shepherd Conservancy describes itself as a "policing body" that enforces international regulations against the illegal slaughter of seals, dolphins, and whales. This group conducts educational programs to increase public awareness of endangered sea animals and also uses such tactics as the blocking, ramming, and sinking of ships that intend harm to sea animals.

The Sea Shepherd Conservancy is an all-volunteer organization and everyone from office personnel to sea captains and mates is a volunteer. For further information, visit the organization's website at www.seashepherd.org or write:

The Sea Shepherd International
P.O. Box 2616
Friday Harbor, WA 98250

Rainforest Action Network (RAN)

The Rainforest Action Network is working to bring the destruction of the world's rain forests to the public's attention through direct actions such as boycotts and information campaigns. RAN has established Rainforest Action groups in 150 locations around the United States, organizing local citizens for nonviolent action.

RAN also coordinates an information network with more than sixty environmental and human rights groups worldwide. RAN offers a number of internships at its main office and at field locations in and around the rain forests of the world.

For further information, visit the website at www.ran.org or contact:

Rainforest Action Network
221 Pine Street
San Francisco, CA 94104

Regional Environmental Resource Centers

The best way to conduct an information search in your area is to contact local environmental organizations. The following is a list of environmental centers located throughout the country that provide information on local and regional environmental issues, jobs, internships, and volunteer opportunities. Each of these organizations can also be found on the Internet.

Ecology Center
2530 San Pablo Avenue
Berkeley, CA 94702
www.ecologycenter.org

Alaska Center for the Environment
519 West Eighth Street
Anchorage, AL 99501
www.akcenter.org

The Ecology Center
801 Sherwood Street #B
Missoula, MT 59802
www.wildrockies.org

Student Environmental Action Coalition
P.O. Box 31909
Philadelphia, PA 19104
www.seac.org

Ecology Center of Ann Arbor
117 North Division Street
Ann Arbor, MI 48104
www.ecocenter.org

Lousiana Environmental Action Network (LEAN)
P.O. Box 66323
Baton Rouge, LA 70896
www.leanweb.org

Volunteer and Internship Organizations

These organizations place students and educators in internships
and volunteer positions all around the country. The following
two have been very successful and have built a good reputation
for placing students in good environmental positions.

Environmental Careers Organization (ECO)

The highly respected Environmental Careers Organization places college students (both undergraduate and graduate) with at least three years of credit in paid intern positions. These jobs last anywhere from three months to two years and, in many cases, lead to employment in the organization. The ECO estimates that 80 percent of its interns are hired after their initial job periods. The majority of jobs are in private companies and government organizations. Intern positions are highly competitive, and only one in eight applicants is placed in a job. There are four regional offices located in Cleveland, Ohio; San Francisco, California; Seattle, Washington; and Tampa Bay, Florida.

In addition, the ECO distributes all types of information on environmental organizations, job-search strategies, and resources. The organization also publishes *The Complete Guide to Environmental Careers in the 21st Century*, which is a valuable book for anyone interested in a science-oriented environmental career.

For an application and more information, visit the website at www.eco.org or contact:

The Environmental Careers Organization
68 Harrison Avenue
Boston, MA 02111

Student Conservation Association (SCA)

The Student Conservation Association offers internships to high school and college students, teachers, senior citizens, and anyone else interested in helping manage public lands in the United States. The SCA has two management programs: the High School Work Group and the Resource Assistance Program.

When writing for information, be sure to specify which of the programs interests you. This group is also active on many college campuses.

The SCA also publishes *Earth Work*, a monthly listing of environmental and natural-resource management jobs, with information on internships and volunteer positions.

For more information, visit the website at www.sca-inc.org or contact:

The Student Conservation Association
P.O. Box 550
Charlestown, NH 03603

Additional Sources of Information

Summer Jobs for Students (annual). Published by Peterson's Guides. More than fifty-five thousand summer jobs at resorts, camps, national parks, and government offices, many with an environmental bent.

The National Directory of Internships (1998). By Gita Gulati and published by the National Society for Experiential Education. This guide describes how to find an intern program that is right for you and how to develop that experience into a career.

Conservation Directory (annual). Published by the National Wildlife Federation. Includes a state-by-state listing of nonprofit volunteer organizations with full descriptions, contact numbers, addresses, and names.

Internships (annual). Published by Peterson's Guides. Lists more than two thousand organizations worldwide.

Environmental Magazines

Magazines, pamphlets, and newsletters are a great source of environmental job information because they list thousands of jobs and intern opportunities every year. Many are monthly or quarterly publications that specialize in environmental issues. Some of these publications are available at local newsstands, and most can be found at local and college libraries or at local environmental organization offices.

E: The Environmental Magazine
Earth Action Network
28 Knight Street
Norwalk, CT 06851

EarthWork
EW Department 517402
Student Conservation Association
P.O. Box 550
Charlestown, NH 03603
  A monthly magazine filled with information on full-time and seasonal jobs in administration/management, education, fieldwork, policy, and research.

Environmental Opportunities
P.O. Box 1253
Edgarton, MA 02539

Environmental Career Opportunities
P.O. Box 678
Stanardsville, VA 22973
www.ecojobs.com

Greenpeace Magazine
702 H Street NW #300
Washington, DC 20001

Opportunity NOC's
TMC
870 Market Street
San Francisco, CA 94102
> A very good weekly listing of nonprofit jobs located throughout the country.

The Job Seeker
Route 2, Box 16
Warrens, WI 54666
> Published biweekly and lists more than two hundred job openings.

Internet Networks and Resources

The growth of on-line environmental information listings has made countless resources instantly available at any time. Most nonprofit organizations, companies, societies, and government agencies maintain Internet sites that highlight the organization's latest information and activities.

Career sites can be an excellent place to obtain information about job opportunities. They provide a forum for employers to list job openings and for individuals to post their resumes. Some Internet sites may also provide the opportunity to research a particular organization to gain greater insights into their goals and and current initiatives.

One outstanding Internet resource is America's Job Bank (AJB), which is administered by the U.S. Department of Labor and lists as many as one million job openings on any given day. These job openings are compiled by state employment service offices throughout the nation. To learn more about AJB, go to www.ajb.dni.us.

CHAPTER SEVEN

Careers in Media

Communicating About the Environment

If you are reading this book, chances are that you consider yourself to be an environmentalist. It could be that you are just beginning the process of educating yourself about the pressing environmental issues at hand or that you know a lot about the environment and are getting ready to make saving our Earth your life's work. No matter what your situation, a large part of your environmental education has come from the media and various other communication sources and not from teachers or national parks.

In almost every major newspaper, there is usually a piece on an environmental issue. Businesses publish literature on the "naturalness" and environmental policies of their organizations, and television advertising sends messages to us about saving our planet. The people who work to continually educate us include journalists for newspapers, magazines, and organizational publications; freelance writers; technical writers; and community relations personnel. These people work at all levels of government, corporations, and consulting firms, and the need for them is growing. In addition, an increasing number of positions are available in electronic media such as radio, television, film, video, and the Internet. In all of these areas, there are numerous other people working to support the green communicator. Researchers, writers, and production staffs all play an important role in spreading the word.

There is an extraordinary amount of information about the environment that needs to be communicated. Each day there are new catastrophes, new findings, new developments, and new policies that need to be presented to the general public. In many cases, the transmission of information is mandated by law in the environmental field. For example, when a major polluter is ordered to clean up its facilities or dump sites, it is required by law to share with the public every detail of its plan for how it is going to go about doing its work. Community right-to-know legislation gives the individual the opportunity to evaluate the risks and hazards associated with any project.

Preparing for a Career as an Environmental Communicator

In preparing for a career as an environmental communicator, you will need to consider the many factors that you would be dealing with on an everyday basis, such as an overwhelming amount of information, sensitive issues, resistance to change, and a growing but relatively new environmental awareness on the part of industrial and corporate America.

Individuals who work in communications generally do not have a technical background. More typically, these individuals have been trained to understand the information needs of the general public or of employees. No matter what the profession, the work demands a willingness to learn continually and an ability to convey oral and written information in an understandable manner. It also requires keeping up on environmental legislation, public opinion about the environment, and new developments in environmentally related areas such as research and development, violations, policies, and trends.

A general bachelor of arts degree in English, sociology, or geography, coupled with an interest in the environment, is one way to prepare yourself. Others may seek more specialized degrees in environmental studies, communications, journalism, technical writing, or marketing. Whatever course of study you pursue, an essential part of your education will be your independent study of environmental issues.

Salaries, while generally and traditionally lower than those in highly technical professions, are reasonable. Starting salaries can range from anywhere in the low twenties to upper thirties, depending on the size of the organization and the level of your experience.

Opportunities in Environmental Communication

The following list of jobs in the communication industry illustrates where opportunities exist and where new opportunities are developing for the career-minded environmentalist. As you will note, some of these careers have not traditionally been considered to be green careers, but your interest and commitment to the environment can make them that way.

Written Communication: News

As you begin your investigation to find an environmental career, you will find yourself buying, reading, saving, and clipping literature from a variety of sources. This information, while educational and informative, is also representative of a possible career. Under the umbrella title of *journalism* exist many opportunities for good writers.

Environmental Reporters

Newspapers, in addition to being an excellent source for names, organizations, agencies, corporations, and individuals to contact in your career planning and job search, also are the source of a new and expanding career. The environmental reporter is some-one who focuses exclusively on writing about the environment. It needs to be noted, however, that presently, this is not where the most jobs are. The New York Times, a newspaper with one of the largest circulations in the country, has only a handful of environmental reporters on staff. Smaller local and community newspapers may cover environmental issues, but the staff reporters cover many areas and do not focus exclusively on the environment.

Environmental Writers: Magazines, Journals, Newsletters

In response to increased concern and desire for information about the state of our Earth, numerous new publications have come into existence that focus exclusively on the environment. Some, like *Biocycle, The Journal of Composting and Recycling*, focus on a specific issue and are very specialized. Others, such as *E: The Environmental Magazine*, are designed to convey infor-mation and news about a wide variety of environmental issues, controversies, and general interest stories.

Most of these publications hire full-time staff writers to produce stories for each issue, whether weekly, monthly, or bimonthly, and numerous freelance writers are called upon to cover and report on special-interest groups and issues.

Whether freelance or full-time, the opportunities for envi-ronmental writers are continuing to grow. The following list of publications and their addresses will give you a general idea of the number, type, and variety of publications that exist today. This list is by no means comprehensive but instead is a sampling of some of the best magazines, journals, newsletters, and organi-zational publications that are available. There are more than one hundred environmental publications in print today. Many of these are available at newsstands, others in libraries, and others directly from the organizations themselves. Addresses have been included for those who are interested in requesting further information, and by using the title of the publication as keywords, you will be able to find most of these on the Internet.

Environmental Publications

Amicus Journal
40 West Twentieth Street
New York, NY 10011

Biocycle, The Journal of Composting and Recycling
The JG Press
419 State Avenue
Emmaus, PA 18049

E: The Environmental Magazine
Earth Action Network
28 Knight Street
Norwalk, CT 06851

Earth First! The Radical Environmental Journal
P.O. Box 1415
Eugene, OR 97490

Earthwork Magazine
Student Conservation Association
P.O. Box 550
Charlestown, NH 03603

Earth Island Journal
300 Broadway, #28
San Francisco, CA 94133

Environmental Business Journal
Environmental Business Publications, Inc.
4452 Park Boulevard, #306
San Diego, CA 92116

Hazardous Waste News
8737 Colesville Road
Silver Spring, MD 20910

In Business, The Magazine for Environmental Entrepreneuring
The JG Press
419 State Avenue
Emmaus, PA 18049

Journal of the Air & Waste Management Association
One Gateway Center
Pittsburgh, PA 15222

Journal of Environmental Health
National Environmental Health Association
720 South Colorado Boulevard, #970 South
Denver, CO 80246

National Parks
National Parks and Conservation Association
1015 Thirty-first Street NW
Washington, DC 20007

Organic Times
New Hope Communication
1301 Spruce Street
Boulder, CO 80302

Science
American Association for the Advancement of Science
1200 New York Avenue NW
Washington, DC 20005

Sierra
85 Second Street, Second Floor
San Francisco, CA 94105

The Earth Times
P.O. Box 3363
Grand Central Station
New York, NY 10163

Whole Earth
1408 Mission Avenue
San Rafael, CA 94901

Written Communication: Books

A new and growing market for environmental literature has opened up as a result of our increased awareness about the state of the Earth. From children's books to reference books to college textbooks, literature about the environment is in demand. The writers of these books come from a multitude of backgrounds, but all the writers have one thing in common—a desire to educate and inform the masses about the problems we face and to pose possible solutions.

The skills required to write books are similar to those needed for any communication career: an interest in the subject, an ability to translate an overwhelming amount of information into a manageable and understandable format, and an ability to meet deadlines. Writing a book also requires that the author have a good sense of what types of literature exist already and a good sense of what people are interested in reading. The following three categories are areas that are publishing more and more about the environment.

Children's Books

Children's book publishing is a very large segment of the publishing industry in America. There are a number of large publishing houses that have children's divisions as well as a number of small, independent presses. Manuscripts for children's books are accepted over the transom, which means that manuscripts or ideas can be sent directly to the publishers without having to hire a literary agent.

If you are interested in writing children's books, you will need to spend some time browsing in bookstores to see what type of literature is being published. You will also want to notice what types of books are coming from what houses and send your manuscript to the publishers that are already publishing environmental literature. The best directory for getting addresses is the *Literary Market Place* (available in the reference section of most libraries).

Trade and Reference Books

A new market has emerged for trade and reference titles that concern themselves with environmental issues—from books on specific environmental issues to books on careers for environmentalists and everything in between. Many of these books are written by experts, by academics, by professionals, and sometimes in conjunction with specific organizations.

Having a good idea coupled with previous writing experience is the beginning of a career as a writer. In many instances, it may be a good idea to work with an agent to find the best home for your project.

Three of the best publishers of environmental literature are Island Press, the Natural Resources Defense Council, and the World Resources Institute.

Island Press, founded in 1978, is a nonprofit organization that publishes books solely on environmental topics. The press currently publishes thirty-five to forty new titles each year and has more than four hundred titles in print. Contact Island Press directly to learn more about submitting a book proposal:

Island Press
Box 7
Covelo, CA 95428

The Natural Resources Defense Council publishes books and papers on environmental issues such as the rain forest, solid waste management, water and air pollution, energy issues, food safety, pesticide use, and experimental education material for children. The NRDC is also an excellent resource for those interested in researching a specific environmental issue. For more information, write:

Natural Resources Defense Council
40 West Twentieth Street
New York, NY 10011

The World Resources Institute does research and assists the government, private sector, and organizations on environmental and management issues. The annual *World Resource Report* is published by the institute and will be a useful source of information for any type of literature that you are considering writing. For more information, write:

World Resources Institute
1750 New York Avenue NW
Washington, DC 20006

College Textbooks

Many disciplines in the college curriculum have courses that deal specifically with environmental issues. In economics departments there are courses in environmental and natural resource economics, and at many institutions an introductory ecology course is offered. In addition, many English instructors are using collections of environmental literature to teach their writing courses. To be qualified to write a college textbook, the author must have a master's degree or doctorate in the discipline. Like children's books, manuscripts for college textbooks are accepted over the transom. *Literary Market Place* (LMP) is the best resource for the addresses of publishers.

Written Communication: Technical Writer

The technical writer, or proposal writer, is the title given to someone who has the responsibility of gathering together technical information from a variety of sources in preparation for making a bid on a government contract. The better written the document, the better the chance of getting the contract. Due to an increase in environmental legislation, in addition to presenting a polished document, it is also essential that it is environmentally focused.

The skills required for this type of work include the ability to convert records and oral reports into finished documents, an eye for detail, and specialized training in technical writing. Many colleges now offer degrees in technical writing, and a variety of courses in technical writing are often offered through English departments.

Electronic Communication: Television, Video, Film, and Internet

The electronic media of television, video, film, and the Internet are all an integral part of conveying environmental messages to the general public. From consultants who are hired to guarantee and protect the locations for shoots to writers and producers of documentaries about nature and the environment, the electronic media are filled with environmentally literate workers. Training for some of these careers is extensive and technical, and the environmental component is often the result of a strong personal interest and desire to work for the benefit of the Earth. Consultants are used to provide the expertise to confirm and polish the messages that will eventually reach a large viewing audience.

Consumer Communication: Advertising

More and more products are hitting the shelves with the green consumer in mind, and advertising is used to let us know about them. Companies that have responded to our pleas for safer products are gaining market share. As a result, advertising agencies are called upon to promote this new consumer greenness. While a few have taken advantage of this consumer trend by promoting products as green when in fact they are not, there does exist a real need for meaningful, effective advertising of environmentally safe products and services. Designers, account executives, and copywriters are all needed to develop and design environmental advertising campaigns.

Goodwill Communication: Community Relations Manager

Community right-to-know laws require manufacturers to reveal detailed information on the expected risks of a cleanup action and on preparing for emergencies near chemical plants, utilities, and other factories. This information is passed to the public through a community relations manager. This is essentially a function of the public relations department. The job require-ments include an ability to communicate and diplomatic and technical skills. An ability to understand scientific and technical data is also a requirement. Most community relation managers work for consulting firms that serve the offending polluters.

The Critical Link: Market Research

Many businesses are interested in increasing their market shares by producing green goods and in gaining the edge in an evolving market. Market researchers are continually probing the con-sumer to find out just how environmentally committed we are. Because of underdeveloped technologies, recycled or green prod-ucts tend to cost more. The most often asked question by researchers is whether consumers are willing to pay a premium for environmental improvement. Individuals who work in market research typically have studied market research and have taken courses in statistics.

State Environmental Protection Agencies

E nvironmental protection agencies oversee the overall quality of the environment by coordinating and managing the state's pollution-control programs and planning, permit granting, and regulation of standards. This is a helpful list of state departments of environmental quality and management.

ALABAMA
Department of Environmental Management
1400 Coliseum Boulevard
P.O. Box 301-463
Montgomery, AL 36130

ALASKA
Department of Environmental Conservation
410 Willoughby Avenue, Suite 105
Juneau, AK 99801

AMERICAN SAMOA (U.S. Territory)
Environmental Protection Agency
Office of the Governor
Pago Pago, AS 96799

ARIZONA
Department of Environmental Quality
3033 North Central Avenue
Phoenix, AZ 85012

ARKANSAS
Department of Environmental Quality
P.O. Box 8913
Little Rock, AR 72219

CALIFORNIA
555 Capitol Mall, Suite 525
Sacramento, CA 95814

COLORADO
Colorado Department of Public Health & Environment
4300 Cherry Creek Drive South
Denver, CO 80246

CONNECTICUT
Division of Environmental Quality
Department of Environmental Protection
79 Elm Street
Hartford, CT 06106

DELAWARE
Department of Natural Resources and Environmental Control
P.O. Box 1401
Dover, DE 19903

DISTRICT OF COLUMBIA
1250 Twenty-third Street NW, Suite 100
Washington, DC 20440

FLORIDA
Department of Environmental Protection
3900 Commonwealth Boulevard, MS-10
Tallahassee, FL 32399

GEORGIA
Environmental Protection Division
Department of Natural Resources
205 Butler Street SW
East Tower, Suite 1152
Atlanta, GA 30334

GUAM (U.S. Territory)
Guam Environmental Protection Agency
15-6101 Mariner Avenue, Tiyan
P.O. Box 22439
Barrigada, GU 96921

HAWAII
Department of Land and Natural Resources
1151 Punchbowl Street
Honolulu, HI 96813

IDAHO
Department of Environmental Quality
1410 North Hilton
Boise, ID 83706

ILLINOIS
Department of Natural Resources
524 South Second Street
Springfield, IL 62701

INDIANA
Department of Environmental Management
100 North Senate Avenue, N1301
Indianapolis, IN 46204

IOWA
Department of Natural Resources
Wallace State Office Building
East Ninth & Grand Avenues
Des Moines, IA 50319

KANSAS
Division of Environment
Forbes Field Building
6700 Southwest Topeka Boulevard
Topeka, KS 66619

KENTUCKY
Department for Environmental Protection
Frankfort Office Park
14 Reilly Road
Frankfort, KY 40601

LOUISIANA
Department of Environmental Quality
P.O. Box 82263
Baton Rouge, LA 70804

MAINE
Department of Environmental Protection
17 State House Station
Augusta, ME 04333

MARYLAND
Department of the Environment
Building 30A, Second Floor
2500 Broening Highway
Baltimore, MD 21224

MASSACHUSETTS
Department of Environmental Protection
One Winter Street
Boston, MA 02108

MICHIGAN
Department of Environmental Quality
P.O. Box 30473
Lansing, MI 48909

MINNESOTA
Environmental Quality Board
658 Cedar Street, Suite 300
St. Paul, MN 55155

MISSISSIPPI
Department of Environmental Quality
2380 Highway 80 West
Jackson, MS 39204

MISSOURI
Department of Natural Resources
Jefferson Building, Twelfth Floor
P.O. Box 176
Jefferson City, MO 65102

MONTANA
Department of Environmental Quality
1520 East Sixth Avenue
P.O. Box 200901
Helena, MT 59620

NEBRASKA
Department of Environmental Quality
1200 N Street, Suite 400
Lincoln, NE 68509

NEVADA
Department of Conservation and Natural Resources
123 West Nye Lane
Carson City, NV 89706

NEW HAMPSHIRE
Department of Environmental Services
P.O. Box 95
Concord, NH 03302

NEW JERSEY
Department of Environmental Protection
401 East State Street
P.O. Box 402
Trenton, NJ 08625-0402

NEW MEXICO
Environment Department
P.O. Box 26110
Santa Fe, NM 87502

NEW YORK
Department of Environmental Conservation
50 Wolf Road
Albany, NY 12233

NORTH CAROLINA
Department of Environment and Natural Resources
P.O. Box 27687
Raleigh, NC 27687

NORTH DAKOTA
Environmental Health Section
Department of Health
P.O. Box 5520
Bismarck, ND 58506

OHIO
Environmental Protection Agency
P.O. Box 1049
Columbus, OH 43216

OKLAHOMA
Department of Environmental Quality
707 North Robinson
Oklahoma City, OK 73102

OREGON
Department of Environmental Quality
811 Southwest Sixth Avenue
Portland, OR 97204

PENNSYLVANIA
Department of Environmental Protection
P.O. Box 2063
Harrisburg, PA 17105

PUERTO RICO (U.S. Territory)
Environmental Quality Board
P.O. Box 11488
San Juan, PR 00910

RHODE ISLAND
Department of Environmental Management
235 Promenade Street, Suite 425
Providence, RI 02908

SOUTH CAROLINA
Environmental Quality Control Office
Department of Health & Environmental Control
2600 Bull Street
Columbia, SC 29201

SOUTH DAKOTA
Department of Environment & Natural Resources
Joe Foss Building
523 East Capitol Avenue
Pierre, SD 57501

TENNESSEE
Department of Environment and Conservation
401 Church Street
Nashville, TN 37243

TEXAS
Natural Resource Conservation Commission
12100 Park 35 Circle, Building A
P.O. Box 13087, MC 109
Austin, TX 78711

U.S. VIRGIN ISLANDS (U.S. Territory)
Department of Planning & Natural Resources
Cyril East King Airport, Second Floor
St. Thomas, VI 00802

UTAH
Department of Environmental Quality
168 North 1950 West
P.O. Box 144810
Salt Lake City, UT 84114

VERMONT
Agency of Natural Resources
103 South Main Street
Waterbury, VT 05671

VIRGINIA
Department of Environmental Quality
629 East Main Street
Richmond, VA 23219

WASHINGTON
Department of Ecology
P.O. Box 47600
Olympia, WA 98504

WEST VIRGINIA
Bureau of Environmental Protection
10 McJunkin Road
Nitro, WV 25143

WISCONSIN
Department of Natural Resources
P.O. Box 7921
Madison, WI 53707

WYOMING
Department of Environmental Quality
122 West Twenty-fifth Street
Cheyenne, WY 82002

About the Authors

Michael Fasulo is a writer, college instructor, and environmental activist. He teaches geography and environmental studies at Truckee Meadows Community College in the Lake Tahoe basin of California. An ardent environmental preservationist, he is a volunteer interpretive naturalist and a member of several environmental action organizations. He is also the author of VGM's *Careers in the Environment*. He earned his bachelor of arts degree in sociology from the University of Wisconsin, Madison, and his master of arts degree in sociology from Pennsylvania State University.

Jane Kinney is a publishing professional who lives and works in New York City. Holding a master of arts degree in Italian literature, she has previously taught Italian at the University of Wisconsin, Madison.

DATE DUE			